A STORY of RESILIENCE

IMMIGRATION, MIGRATION AND TRAUMA OF SUB-SAHARA AFRICAN WOMEN IN CANADA

EDITH NGENE KAMBERE

Order this book online at www.trafford.com
or email orders@trafford.com

Most Trafford titles are also available at major online book retailers.

Print information available on the last page.

ISBN: 978-1-4907-8017-7 (sc)
ISBN: 978-1-4907-8019-1 (hc)
ISBN: 978-1-4907-8018-4 (e)

Library of Congress Control Number: 2017900275

Trafford rev.   06/21/2017

www.trafford.com

North America & international
toll-free: 1 888 232 4444 (USA & Canada)
fax: 812 355 4082

CONTENTS

FOREWORD

I have known Edith Ngene Kambere for 20 years. In 1996 we met in a focus group that I organized as part of a research project on settlement issues facing recent immigrant women in Canada. Edith spoke passionately about her own experiences as a newcomer to Canada, and her observations about what was happening to other African women she was working with as a settlement counselor. From our first meeting it was evident to me that Edith is an extraordinarily strong and perceptive woman. Little did I know then that our meeting would result in a deep and lasting friendship that would also change the course of my research, which soon shifted to focus on the local African diaspora, and shift my volunteer activities to a longstanding involvement with Umoja Operation Compassion Society that includes travelling together back to the village of Rwentutu in western Uganda, where Edith's story began.

The first half of Edith's memoire documents her early life in Rwentutu. Her father's unusual emphasis on educating his daughters along with his sons instilled in Edith a determination to pursue higher education, a promise eventually fulfilled much later in Canada. She remembers with pride her role as the young wife of a new member of parliament, and the pleasure that brought in working with local women in community development. More traumatic was the overthrow of the government that sent her husband Amos to jail and then into exile. Edith recounts the incredible hardships of a young mother coping alone with small children in a now hostile and dangerous Uganda, leaving her oldest son, then only 3, with relatives when she fled to Congo, and the struggles of eking out an existence in the years before she was able to rejoin all her children and her husband in Kinshasa. The trauma of refugee life is evident throughout these pages, but so too is Edith's resilience and the friendship of other women and men who helped her along the way.

When they were finally resettled in Vancouver Canada through the UNHCR in May of 1992, I am sure Edith and Amos hoped the worst was over. But what followed was a long period of depression linked to post traumatic stress disorder, compounded by the difficulties of adjusting to a new society. Slowly, Edith drew on her own resilience, improved her English, got her high school equivalency, began to take university courses, and found work as a settlement counselor helping other African women adjust to life in Canada. The collective trauma that marks refugee experiences and the many settlement obstacles encountered in Canada would later become the subject of Edith's MSW thesis. In her memoire she weaves together her own story with the narratives of other women to highlight common themes and to make recommendations for how settlement counselors and social workers can better help immigrants and refugees overcome trauma.

When I met Edith in that focus group in 1996 she was already taking university courses with the hope of getting a Bachelor's degree. Over the next six years, from 1996-2002, I interviewed Edith and her husband Amos every year and chronicled the changes in their lives as they juggled the demands of work, family and integration into a new culture and society for themselves and their four sons. Over the years we talked about the difficulties of not having extended family near by, the work of building community in a new place, facing discrimination based on race and accents, pursuing new educational opportunities and developing careers, and the pleasure in becoming home owners. Parenting was always uppermost in these conversations, since raising four young Black boys in a city where they were often the only Black children in their schools and neighbourhoods, was a significant challenge. And always, every time we met Edith would say "you have to do some research on the issues facing African women".

When Edith completed her undergraduate degree - a major feat while navigating a new culture, working to help pay the bills, and raising four young sons - we did begin to conduct research together. Beginning with focus groups with African women, followed by in-depth interviews with men and women to chart the uneven terrain of settlement and belonging, and later still, focus groups with immigrant and refugee youth from African countries, Edith became my research assistant and collaborator. In the process, Edith also attained a Masters Degree in Social Work and embarked on a new career. But she never left behind her commitment to help other immigrants and refugees navigate the hardships of migration. Together with her husband Amos, and a small group of others from the local African Diaspora, Umoja Operation Compassion Society was born. For more than a decade now Umoja has operated as a settlement organization in the suburb of Surrey, providing programs for newcomers with a particular focus on mothers, children and youth. Through her work as a settlement counselor, then a social worker, and her tireless volunteer labour for Umoja, Edith has always worked to make her new home a better place for others.

True to the beginning of this story, Umoja has a second focus of improving the lives of families in their home village of Rwentutu in western Uganda. Edith and Amos donated land they own in Rwentutu and raised funds and volunteers to build and run an elementary school for local girls and boys, to develop a micro finance program for village women, and to build and run a medical clinic on the school grounds. It was a trip to visit the school and the women who participate in the micro credit program that brought Edith and I back to Uganda and the village of Rwentutu in 2009, as members of the Board of Umoja documenting the impact of Umoja's activities in Rwentutu. Through building infrastructure and community development in Rwentutu, Edith and Amos have come full circle to their early days as they sought to better the lives of villagers in their home community.

As you will see in the pages that follow, Edith's memoire includes much heartache and trauma, but is ultimately the story of recovery, resilience and significant personal accomplishments that have a positive impact in both societies, Uganda and Canada, that she now calls home.

Gillian Creese
Professor, Sociology Department and the Institute for Gender, Race, Sexuality & Social Justice, University of British Columbia
October 2, 2016

PREFACE

It is with much pleasure that I sit down to write the preface for my book. In the 25 years since I first came to Canada with my family much has changed in the treatment of refugees and immigrant women who have come from war torn countries. Although things are improving, not many African women have had the opportunity to share their personal memories and experiences, and to tell service providers and counselors how African women should be treated. This book, written from the perspective of both an insider and an outsider, tries to fill that gap by building on the need for greater compassion, sensitivity and empathy.

Telling my experiences of trauma, strength and resilience, and sharing stories of other African women, provides lessons that will be useful for immigration officers, professionals in mental health, social workers, teachers and other professionals and clinicians who work with immigrant and refugee women, helping them to discover new ways of sensitively handling trauma. Therefore, it is my hope that this book will be useful for counselors in schools, social workers in practice, and health and settlement workers of all kinds who might benefit from more knowledge about how to work with immigrants and refugees suffering the effects of pre- and post-migration traumas. It is my desire that this book will help clinicians to reflect on and learn from these narratives, in the process building a stronger foundation that will foster the healing process.

ACKNOWLEDGEMENTS

As I conclude the chapter of writing my first book, I would like to take a moment to extend my sincere gratitude to many people who have helped me through the process from commencement up to the finishing point.

To begin, the more I thought about writing this acknowledgement section, the more I grasped that the people I have known throughout my life journey in Uganda, the Democratic Republic of Congo, and Canada, and what they have contributed in writing this book.

First of all, I am ever grateful to my dear brother, Dr. Mambo Masinda, who from the beginning of my masters studies, encouraged me to write a book based on my personal experience, and the work that I have been involved in working with immigrant women. I would like also to express my very sincere gratitude to Dr. Pilar Riano-Alcala and Dr. Gillian Creese for holding my hands in pursuing my higher education.

I would like to express my very sincere gratitude to Dr. Kathryn Bernard for her attention to details and observations. Her advice was truly instrumental. I acknowledge my gratitude to my sister Thoko Barbara Kuehn. Without her, this book would not have been possible. She prayed and reminded me of how vividly it was like living in those circumstances described in this book.

I am infinitely grateful to the 13 women participants who shared their personal painful experiences with me. In the course of their willingness to share their stories, this book became a reality. It is very unfortunate that our sister Bayushi who was part of this group was tragically killed by a woman she was caring for. May her soul rest in peace. I am indebted to the support I received from many sisters and brothers during my exile in the Congo.

I am grateful to my boys. They prayed for me when I could not move a step ahead. Their experiences of waiting for me to come from school at night, taking care of each other have become a back born of my pride as a mother. My only wish for you boys is to continue my passion in the very best way you can as I have seen you go the root of helping others because we were also helped through our journey of exile and migration.

My very sincere thanks go to my husband, Amos Mubunga Kambere who has been a rock for me in completing this book. Thank you for believing in my strengths as a social worker and a mother! No words are enough to express my gratitude for your support in this project.

Finally, I take this opportunity to express the profound gratitude from my deep heart to my beloved parents Elisha and Elizabeth Mulima and my siblings for their love and continuous support. Thank you for being wonderful family members who enabled me to write a book that will be read by many folks, and hopefully help heal their hurts.

Edith Ngene-Kambere, MSW RSW

INTRODUCTION

The writer of this script holds a Masters degree in Social Work, and a Registered Social Worker (MSW, RSW), working in one of the mental health institutions in Fraser Health Authority, British Colombia. As an African Immigrant Woman, who arrived in Canada from Uganda over 24 years ago, how did I get there? Walk with me as I share my journey of great aspiration for education and bumps that I encountered. It is a story of some self-determination which could never come through without the support that I received from the community.

Some of the readers may ask themselves why I have decided to share my life story. It has been demonstrated that personal story narratives can help individuals get connected to their past and even figure out how to deal with daily socioeconomic and emotional conditions. More importantly, they can help people listening or reading them feel connected and a sense of not being alone in their struggles and aspirations. Stories constitute a bank of knowledge which can be used as healing of others' wounds. It is with that trust that I want to welcome women who come from different walks of life who have experienced atrocities and professionals who work with them to read my story.

It is my deepest hope that after you have read my story you will feel that it is not too late to accomplish your dream and be the woman that you have always wanted to be!! Do not listen to that person who has judged you by the way you look, speak, or dress. Look at yourself and feel the delight in you and say, "I am valued, I am beautiful, I am smart, and I can make it, no matter what." I am where I am today because there were people who believed in me and some of those who were my role models.

In this book, I weave together my personal story of my struggles growing up in an African culture at a time when education for girls was given little consideration, and stories of other women's traumatic stories caused by political violence; our small miracles which sustained our hopes during the pains endured during the pre and post immigration processes. The book offers knowledge and insight to professionals who work closely with immigrant women struggling with social, cultural and economic challenges in the process of integration into their communities in Canada.

Although my experience is not unique among other immigrant women's stories, it has given me a reason to appreciate each day that God blesses me with life, shelter, freedom from gun shots, and an abundance of resources. I am ever grateful that as immigrants and professional workers read this book which is an interweaving of the comments of African immigrant women, excerpts from my own personal story, and the insights of others, they will encounter new perspectives about African Immigrant Women.

The book is divided into 4 sections. In the first section, I present the methodology and my process of writing this narrative. The second deals with the pre-migration socio-economic and political contexts in Uganda and the conditions of my refugee life in the Democratic Republic of Congo (DRC). In the third section, I elaborate on my post-immigration experience, thus the process of integrating into the Canadian society. The fourth part is about what I consider to be some pre-requisites professionals working with African immigrant women and other women with similar experiences should keep reflecting upon in the course of their work.

The book is a combination of my own story and other African immigrant women's pre and post immigration stories to validate the interconnections between the past and the present on one hand, and on the other hand exemplify the power of the community support in helping individuals heal from their trauma. In her presentation on July 15, 2008, Dr. Adele Diamond made the following assertion:

The longer I live, the more I realize the impact of attitude on life. Attitude, to me, is more important than facts. It is more important than the past, than education, than money, than circumstances, than failures, than successes, than what other people think or say or do. It is more important than appearances, giftedness or skill. It will make or break a company, a church, a home. The remarkable thing is you have a choice every day regarding the attitude you will embrace for that day. We cannot change our past. We cannot change the fact that people will act in a certain way. We cannot change the inevitable. The only thing we can do is play on the one string we have, and that is our attitude.

These words have stayed with me, even as I recount my experiences of both countries I call home: Uganda and Canada. After adjusting and readjusting, I am confident that I have come to a place where I am able to name my experiences constructively so that they may prove helpful both to other African immigrant women and to the various professionals who work with them. Keep your hopes high; you will certainly walk to your dreams no matter the bumps on your roads to your aspirations.

Section I

Methodology

I have to make this clear that this is not an academic book in a traditional way meaning proposing a thesis with a line of arguments. It is an academic book considering the story narratives and perspective of developing knowledge.

However, mapping the life experiences of immigrant and refugee women presents a series of transitions and each stage presents numerous challenges as well as opportunities. Every moment, these women must make decisions that will forever change their lives. While every step they go through carries uncertainties, each woman is hopeful that life will be better.

This study captures the journey of 13 women of diverse Sub-Saharan African cultural backgrounds, from their home country to this new homeland, Canada. Their joys and pains, hopes and fears, are narrated from their point of view as experiences of overcoming horrific experiences in two or more different ways.

I chose to use narratives as a knowledge gathering tool because it is an interpretive approach in the social sciences which involves storytelling methodology (Basset & Stickley, 2010). The story of the subject or participant becomes an object of study, focusing on how individuals make sense of events and actions in their lives. In this study, our shared voices have connected us together as women who share similar journeys that have made us strong. In our struggles, we have found a common thread of identifying with one another through the stories and voices that we all share, and we see ourselves as victims and strong in the ways that we have survived our ordeals. We want to build on our traumas and pains for the future generations that come after us for them to know that there is hope even amidst disappointments and trials.

To us as survivors of war trauma, in our home countries as well as in refugee camps in different countries of exile, our stories are a recollection of pain in both home and country of refuge. Some of the women's fondest recollections are of what life back in Africa was like. Particularly they found strength and support from a community that lived collectively rather than an individualistic life. Reflecting on life during crisis brings back painful memories of war, flight, and danger. Life in Canada brings up stories of both challenges and uncertainty in a new environment including women's thoughts on what Canada has in store for them especially the challenges of lack of understanding of their trauma from the professionals and from the employers and coworkers.

Focus groups and one interview were organized in conjunction with participatory research action on "What causes the Mental Health Problems in African Women?" Interested participants were sent a letter that introduced them to this project. I conducted the interview and focus groups and transcribed the information. Of the thirteen African women interviewed, all respondents identified themselves as having suffered some traumatic experiences as a result of war trauma and displacement.

However, some of them show some resiliency in dealing with experiences of trauma. Three-quarters of the women who participated in this study identified themselves as currently married; one was divorced, or, in a handful of cases, never married. Almost all (60%) of women were parents. Only 3 participants identified themselves as neither married nor parents. I did not ask participants about their sexual orientation but in the course of the interview and focus groups, almost all made it apparent they were, or had been, married and/or involved with opposite-sex partners.

It is important to note that the participants in focus groups for this book originated from 7 different countries in Sub-Saharan Africa, namely: Sudan, Sierra Leon, Rwanda, Burundi, Ethiopia, Uganda and the Democratic Republic of Congo. In this project, three of the participants are themselves counselors. One works in mainstream organization counseling battered women, two of these participants work with NGOs that provide services for immigrant women who are victims of spouse abuse, [unfortunately, one of these counselors was murdered in 2013 while in the course of doing what she loved doing for women, before this book got to be published].

Two participant counselors had a university degree; another one had a non-social work degree from her country of origin, and with her social work degree near completion. The third counselor had a community certificate in counseling. The rest of the women had their education outside Canada. One focus group was conducted in Swahili, one of the widely spoken African languages that I speak, which I later translated in English. Two of the focus groups and one interview were conducted in

English. All the focus groups and interviews were transcribed. The core questions were:

- What kind of pre-migration traumatic experiences did you have before arriving in Canada and how did this impact your integration process?
- How has the experience (s) of pre-migration if any interfere with your current health, emotional and physical well-being?
- What traumatic symptoms have you experienced as a result of these experiences?

The three counselors that participated in this group have been my acquaintances for the last 16 years and were primarily contacted on the basis of our prior work experiences with African immigrant women from war-torn countries as well as on the basis of their knowledge about the issues that concern this particular group. The women participants were selected according to the duration of the period in the host country and in particularly from African war-troubled countries. I was very cognizant in getting the participants in this group from a variety of Sub-Saharan African, and to get service providers whose experiences of being victims of trauma has helped them to work effectively in helping Sub-Saharan African Immigrant and Refugee women (AIR) that live in the Vancouver metropolitan area.

This use of "narrative as a research tool" (NRT) was not aimed at discovering what causes mental health problems among AIR women. But a review of the transcribed information from the focus groups and interview indicate to me that they might provide a rich set of data for documenting such findings, as the women's narratives demonstrate. As I understood the study of Narrative as Research tool, I immediately realized that this approach would help me as the author and the readers to learn from the women's stories and recommendations they make.

With this in mind, I came to realize that with an NRT approach of storytelling positions narrative research largely within the postmodernist paradigm. This approach emphasizes that knowledge is value-laden, and reality is based on multiple perspectives, with truth grounded in everyday life involving social interactions amongst individuals. Research indicates that this approach actually captures social representation processes such as feelings, which I was able to witness through the women's narratives. In this study, I got a sense of how narrative can aid education (Abma, 2000;

Cox, 2001), thus how it can act as a source of understanding (Cortazzi, 2001) women's current situations. I came to understand that women's stories told within their cultural contexts to promote certain values and beliefs can contribute to the construction of individual identity.

In taking this approach of storytelling, I needed to be informed on how to listen to the women while trying to help them deal with their own issues of trauma (Ambrosini and Bowman, 2001 and Linde 2001) while reflecting on my own internal turmoil that might still need some healing. Through narratives, told within their cultural contexts this could contribute to the construction of their individual identity or concept of their African community. Storytelling can help in transferring complex tacit knowledge or can also serve as a source of implicit communication. Other aspects include: how narrative can aid education (Abma, 2000; Cox, 2001), how stories contribute to sense-making and how narrative may act as a source of understanding (Cortazzi, 2001) one's internal conflict. While this is the nature of the approach, it is clear that there are also other key attributes of NRT that distinguish it from common problem-solving approaches that we all engage in curing everyday life challenges!

Throughout the women's narrative, they identified four migration stages at which they felt significant potential for trauma experiences that lead to serious psychological distress: 1) pre-migration trauma, such as what they experienced prior to migration to Canada, that were a major factor of leaving their countries of origin; 2) they also described traumatic events experienced during transition to their new country; 3) they highlighted continuing trauma experiences during the process of refugee asylum and re-settlement; and 4) there was mention of mistreatment by professionals and employers in the host country due to either their accent or unknown reasons to these women, inadequate supports, and minority persecution.

The objective of this study was to give the African immigrant and refugee women the opportunity to share their personal life stories of immigrating to Canada, while they inform the service providers on how to better serve them while they integrate into the Canadian society. In this script, I felt the need to target the service providers, mental health professionals, social workers and psychologists because they are the groups of people that AIR Women usually get in close proximity with as soon as they land their feet on their new home, Canada.

The findings in this text report a myriad of complex emotional and physical tasks that must be accomplished by people who leave their homelands. The women's loss of family, community, emotional trauma, and physical environment are themes that echo through both clinical and much research that has been done previously. The loss of familiar social networks is especially hard on families and these AIR women, who often find themselves isolated, are forced to deal on their own with the multiple demands of life in a foreign environment (Masinda and Kambere, 2008; Kambere, 2004; Kleinman, 1995). Unfortunately, this is often a bitter surprise for those women who come with hopes of fresh horizons in a country of new opportunities.

SECTION II

FROM UGANDA TO EXILE IN THE CONGO

※

This section elaborates on my life conditions as a young girl and a woman in Uganda and the subsequent refugee status in the Democratic Republic of Congo.

My life in Uganda

Locating gender in an African cultural setting

My intention of writing this section is to provide context. I begin with my childhood life to inform the readers about the determination that sometimes children have at an early age which can be a motivation factor for them in their adult life. Readers have to understand that when a child is given an opportunity to be loved, encouraged and motivated no matter their weakness, you will be surprised what children grasp in their young life and what they can achieve.

I come from a family and cultural backgrounds that have their own values and beliefs that have contributed to who I am today. Having come from such backgrounds and belief systems, I am ever grateful for the way my character was shaped by challenges and aspirations that I faced as a result. Many of us come from families where we might have faced challenges that were not of our own making. Some of us grew up with aspirations that were motivated by our parents or our own siblings. Others still might have had ambitions and aspirations that would need someone to motivate them for their dreams to become a reality. In other cases, some of us have become the mentors that siblings we grew up with have emulated.

I grew up in a culture where being a first born can be very rewarding, but at the same time very challenging, because everyone looks up to you in order to reach their own goals. The challenge of growing up as the first born in the family is not an easy task, especially if there are no role models in the community that you would emulate. However, in many aspects, it is very rewarding because it shapes the real you to explore many skills that come with being the first child whom the parents and young siblings could rely on for simple house-hold tasks. There are rewards and challenges that one endures by carrying such a place in many of my African cultures. I grew up at a time when girls were not given much consideration in the area of education. Fortunately for me, my parents had a different perspective about girls' education. They were determined to educate their daughter against all odds.

I had three step-siblings younger than me, and two biological siblings - a brother and sister. We were five girls in the family at the time. Having this sizeable number of girls was something that was not perceived well by the community. My father endured all sorts of questioning and mocking from the community members about why he had the audacity to educate his daughters. Some could not understand how a man could have only girls and yet still love them enough to educate them. This was sweet music in my father's ears as he now narrates the story to us grown up daughters. My father saw education as the only investment that he could give his daughters.

Growing up in the late 1960s and 70s, personal success for a girl was secondary. Girls were perceived as second-class citizens and of less value because when they get married, all the wealth would go to someone else- the future husband. My parents never looked at this as an issue that would stop them from educating their girls; instead, they were determined to support us if we chose to study. As the eldest daughter in the family, I was faced with the challenge of beating these odds of everyone expecting me to be the role model for my siblings. As it was the norm in the community, I was also expected to be my parents' pride and joy, which is true in a sense.

The pressure was mounting, but with determination that my siblings should learn from me and emulate what I did, I tried to work harder in my academic aspirations. I was determined to be a leader, a head and not the tail. My father constantly told us that whoever loved to study, he would support them despite the hardships of the financial constraints to raise school fees for nine children, including the four boys that were in the family. With the encouragement I got from my father to be educated, I chose to be that woman who was willing to study no matter the obstacles.

My father was constantly approached by village men who asked him why he was interested in educating girls; he vehemently told them "it was none of their business, and that his money was specifically for his children regardless of whether they were girls." What a man! I salute you, Dad! Everyone who comes from a culture where girls are mostly undervalued and regarded as second class citizen understands what I am talking about here. Growing up in such cultures, it was a matter of proving to the community that one deserves to be valued, and to be a determined person who was willing to thrive no matter the odds. I was determined to be a "woman of status" no matter the obstacles. The concept of being considered a girl who would be property for the husband that I would marry was remote for me.

Besides, I had no intentions of even getting married, so that was no issue for me. However, this self-prophesy was false because I got to be fiancée to my husband when I was only seventeen! I will explain this later. I grew up with a dislike of being undervalued and considered a second class citizen in the society. I wanted to be respected and recognized as someone that brought value and pride to the community in which I grew up. I also wanted to be perceived as someone whose usefulness was to be involved in the lives of others. I had no preconceived ideas of how this would develop into a passion of working with women who come from a similar culture as mine.

Before these ambitions, I recall at an early age, I had wanted to be a "woman of status"! How could this be in the mind of a little girl who was only ten years at the time? God knows what I was longing for. I remember at the age of eight, I started practicing standing in front of an audience addressing other children, demonstrating to them that I was a teacher. Each time my parents and I visited some relatives, the first thing I did was to assemble all of the children around and start addressing them as a means of being a leader or teacher to them. As time went by, my younger brother, my sister and I grew up knowing that the only way we could make our parents proud and happy was to really go an extra mile to be successful in life. In fact, I walked about ten miles back and forth from school. I set my sights on being an achiever, studying and making it to university. I needed to focus on achieving higher and get my objectives of being a "woman of status" in order to win the confidence of my family and the village as a whole. Indeed, I made it, after experiencing major obstacles along the way.

To want to be a woman of "status", you have to work at it and prove to the people around you that you can do it, and that it is possible no matter how much you may fail along the road. It is well documented that people who have made it in life failed many times, provided they never gave up. They maintained their focus and were determined to be who they wanted to be. Like one person puts it regarding former president of the United States of America, Abraham Lincoln:

> He slowly won his way to eminence and fame doing the work that lay next to him—doing it with all his growing might—doing it as well as he could, and learning by his failure, when failure was encountered, how to do it better (Greeley, 2007).

The roots of my passion for education

I come from a family where extended family is the norm. I grew up at a time (in the 1970s) where a woman's education was a non-entity as mentioned earlier in this script. In my young mind, I had this ambition to change the course, to be one of the first ones to change this mentality. I grew up in a society that did not give much regard to women, let alone their education. I had such aspirations of wanting to be one of the few girls that went beyond secondary school. More especially, I wanted to be a leader who would lead other women to reach their aspirations. That is what I had perceived as "woman of status". In my early years, in the 1970s, a woman of "status" was that one who was married to a teacher and owned a car!" These were my ambitions and indeed I got them before I even turned 25 years of age. At the time, being a teacher was the highest qualification imaginable and owning a car was perceived as being the richest person on earth.

Growing up as the first-born daughter was challenging and yet fulfilling in many ways. I became passionate about school and became a competitive young girl. There are of course many different reasons why education became my weapon to achieve my goal of becoming that "woman of status." How could this be for a child who grew up in a rural area where there were no role models that a young girl like me would want to emulate?

For instance, at age eight, before I could even understand the value of education, my parents sent me to go and live with my aunt in another rural area, several miles from home. I went and studied there in grade two. I recall my first day in school; I was the only young and small girl in the class. I missed my mother a lot. I was confused, did not know what to do, but only went to school for the sake of it. Life was not the best because, I missed the love and touch of my mother! After a few semesters at this new school, I was transferred to a different one.

This change from school to school affected my performance in class. Each time I felt I had established a social network of friends, I found myself moved to a different school. Establishing new friendships was also a factor that affected my coping skills. I am that kind of person who does not do well with any change of environment. Getting acquainted with the new teacher's teaching would take me a lot of coping.

There were of course feelings of rejection and of being unloved, as is usually the case when a child is removed from their familiar surroundings. I developed some feelings of insecurity as a result of these disruptions. I could not understand why my parents Chose to send me miles from their care. Besides, my aunt only had one child to look after. I was informed that I was going to help my aunt with this one child and some house chores. Really! Was this important for parents who only had three children of their own to look after?

Besides, I was still a child myself to be looked after at the age of 8, at least as I currently see it by the Western culture's standard. This separation was the most traumatic and troubling experience that I still vividly recall even to this day. I would be asked to go and deliver messages from my aunt to some relatives who lived in the remote area of the mountain, quite a distance from where my aunt lived. In the 60s, the means of communication was very difficult. There was no luxuries of texting or telephone communication. The only means was letter writing, which would be delivered to the recipient by sending kids such as in my case.

Such means of communication meant for me missing school for a day. Some of the mail or verbal message deliveries, was on many occasions under heavy rains, and travelling alone through isolated remote areas from my aunt's house to those relatives. I do not recall a time when I expressed my frustration of this arrangement with my aunt. During my three years of staying away from my parents, and the lack of understanding from my aunt about all that I experienced, I had never demonstrated any hostility towards her or how I felt. In her book *Breaking Free from Spiritual Strongholds*, Moore (2000) articulates some of the insecurities that we all face. She points out that:

"Minor insecurities can be little more than occasional challenges, but when life suddenly erupts like a volcano, insecurity turns into panic. Want suddenly feels like a need. A hidden pocket of unmet needs suddenly quakes and leaves a cavern. The fear or the feeling of being unloved is probably our greatest source of insecurity, whether or not we can always articulate it (p. 89)".

I recall after two years of living away from my parents, I resorted to building my own empire of bottling my pain, a defense mechanism of not wanting to ever go back to my parents. I felt that they had abandoned me, thus believing the lie that they only wanted someone to take care of me. Likewise, I believe many people who have had disruptions in their early life or even in their adult life might attest to this experience. Childhood life is vital because it shapes one's way to withstand the challenges of tomorrow. With me, I believe there were lessons that I learnt during this period that have shaped me to be able to cope with my present social life. I now have a different perspective of viewing children or people whose lives have been disrupted no matter their age when this happened to them. I am more empathetic to my own son who was left behind when he was only three years old at the time I fled my home country-Uganda. I am a more understanding person based on the experience of my childhood.

The illusions of being unloved are far from the truth. Looking back, I missed school most of the time because I was frequently asked to go and do chores for my aunt. I suspect my father who loved to educate his children was happy that his daughter was somewhere studying. He had no clue that this re-location had affected my school performance and my entire childhood life. This whole situation reflects the danger of removing a young child from the mother at such a tender age, when she could not make decisions for herself. I needed to study, but the opportunity was very limited. The disruption took precedent over what I had gone to do. Bear in mind, it is normal in my culture for a young child to go and live with a relative, to help with house chores or to look after the young ones. In my case, this was the arrangement, but with anticipation that I would continue with my schooling.

After three years with my aunt, I went back to my parents and started school in grade two and started over again. It is very important to understand that one of the most difficult things children must deal with is the "lies that can come into their minds masquerading as truth:

I am not loved, I am not accepted, I am not appreciated, I am not good enough" (Omartian, p. 45). Because of the trauma that I had gone through as a young child of only 8 and coming back to my parents after three years, all sorts of lies had built up in my little mind. These lies remained into my teenage years and even into adulthood! I had been called a "failure" and felt totally rejected by my parents for sending me to go and live at such a distance at such tender age.

I believed those lies which had penetrated deep into my mind by my aunt, were indeed true! What I recall now is that I knew how to store such memories in the back of my mind. What I should say is that I placed these thoughts in my "*recycled mind bin*", and later in my adulthood, these memories resurfaced! Each time I had unpleasant situations at work where my accent was criticized for example, or someone speaks to me in a demeaning manner, I would begin to play the ugly words that were spoken to me in my childhood. As well, in my adult life, I do feel scared when someone superior tells me that they would like to meet me; if they are not specific about the meeting. Because this is how I was dealt with when I lived with my aunt. Whenever I had a meeting with her, it was to scold and tell me everything wrong with my character.

Charles Stanley writes "how adults have a tendency to hang on to hurts" (July 2007; p.40). This has been the case in my life when I went through some of my own emotional experiences as an adult. It reminds me that we humans in our nature have different ways of defending ourselves from any pains, especially if we have had ugly experiences growing up. Stanley further points out that "young children generally do not hold grudges. They will react to an unpleasant situation and then let it go" (p.40). The statement above is reflective of what I sometimes felt when I lived with my aunt. There were times when I heard her talk to her village women friends that she marveled at what a cheerful a girl I was. Even after getting a good scolding from her, a few minutes later, I would go my way and continue to do my usual house-chores without showing on my face anything that was displeasing.

When I look back I wonder whether this was a good coping mechanism for dealing with frustration, disappointment, rejection and emotional stress. It is true that some of us have felt rejection in one way or another. Some have found it difficult to let go of those emotional hurts of rejection. Unfortunately, the more we hung on to these pains, the more we get hurt and angry at the perpetrators. Moore (2000) reminds us of how rejection can be a prison of its own. She points out that:

> Few of us will embrace the difficult challenge of being rejected...
> children who have allowed themselves to be imprisoned by
> continuing feelings of rejection for the rest of their lives... I would
> never imply that getting over rejection is easy; but it is possible
> for every [woman and child] who puts her heart and mind to it to
> overcome (p.111).

Sometimes I regret that I did not show my frustrations; upon reflection, maybe this would have helped me heal quicker. John Gray's (1999) words resonate deeply with me. ...if you felt abandoned as a young child, those feelings can still be affecting you. As soon as someone rejects you a little, it can seem much more painful because of your past. When this is the case, the best way to process is to link what you feel now to something you felt then (p.142).

I wonder whether this is a good thing to do now, or whether it has helped me as I have continued to deal with many of life's challenges. Herman (1997) writes:

> A secure sense of connection with caring people is the foundation
> of personality development. When this connection is shattered,
> the traumatized person loses her basic sense of self...the
> developing child's positive sense of self depends upon a caregiver's
> benign use of power. When a parent, who is so much more
> powerful than a child, nevertheless shows some regard for that
> child's individuality and dignity, the child feels valued and
> respected; she develops self-esteem (p.52).

When a child has not had such a caring and supportive environment, being judged in every aspect, there will always be scars of unsatisfactory resolution of the normal developmental conflicts, which may leave the child with a long lasting effect of shame and doubting him/herself.

Although I unconsciously developed a mechanism of maintaining a happy face even when there were pains of rejection, feeling unloved and, of course, missing parental care, these mechanisms have become a catalyst to remain positive even in tough situations. My childhood struggles may have been very traumatic in different respects. However, when I look back, I see that there are new ways, ideas that I have developed in my professional work on how to react, relate, or respond to the needs of the heartbroken women, children, youth and even couples that have struggled with rejection or betrayal by their partners.

The only difference is that my childhood was disrupted by removing me from parental care. The fact remains that pain will always be the same no matter the dimensions of the circumstances of our suffering. The lessons I now see out of my experience is the obstacle that must be conquered, the problem of individual people's inability to understand what disruption does to their inner being. Unfortunately, many well-meaning people attempt to help their hurting friends by uttering words such as: "Get on with your life, don't dwell on your past hurts." Yes, easier said than done. Each of us humans have different ways of dealing with pains. The only hand that one could give in such circumstance is to be empathetic, not judgmental to those people that have had their life disrupted in one way or another.

Let me demonstrate this point more from my experience. My three years of not being in an environment that provided nurturing and affectionate love, meant that my academic pursuit was put on a halt. Still, I did not allow myself to be stuck between the old life and the new life once I rejoined my parents. I am not sure I was conscious of what the two environments had meant for me. All I know is that when my ordeal ended, I met with a man who became my mentor and believed in me, my father. He became inspirational from the moment he received me back into his care (Este & Bernard (2006).

I need to elaborate here that I never shared anything negative with my parents. It is in the summer 2015 when my parents visited me in my now home country Canada, that for the first time I shared my childhood experience with them; some of the pains I had experienced, things I had never shared with anyone. I asked them about how they came with the arrangement of removing their first child from their love at such tender age. My parents were naïve about how this arrangement was reached. They only regretted for having sent me away from their care, and I was able to forgive them after over 40 years of keeping silent!

I knew that I had now overcome this crisis of separation from my parents and was ready to face a new life with my family that loved me and believed in me! My first semester gave me a boost. In the culture where I grew up, the school system works in such a way that students are ranked according to positions in class. They are ranked from number one to the last. This kind of education system gives students a competitive incentive where each student works harder to their fullest in order to be recognized as the highest in school, class or community. I was very competitive by nature because of the training I had received, wanting to win people's acceptance by walking an extra mile. Not only did I want to excel and be a "woman of status", I wanted to ensure that no one in my village looked down upon me, despite women being valued as second-class citizens.

Since I had been made to believe I was a failure by my aunt, I attributed any small set back in my class performance, to my perceived poor performance. This had been securely engraved in my mind that I was incompetent and more so, unworthy. Joel Osteen (2005) says, "One of the most important bits of information that you need to reinstall in your mental computer is that you are a victor and not a victim" (p.135).

I wished there were times when these words were real to me. It was my father who really spoke these words in many instances when he saw my frustrations. I love that man! Sincerely, what I needed was to have someone tell me I was worthy. I was an achiever, but needed confirmation from other people around me who knew how hard I tried to achieve my goal. If there were people who motivated me beyond my own ambitions, I would never have created such mental and physical problems for myself to the point of developing ulcers. I really needed someone that would boost my morale, especially looking at the experience of going to school early in the morning on an empty stomach!

Given that my father was one of the few men in the community who dared educate his daughters against all cultural odds, he had fears of his own as well. If his daughter did not perform well what could he do? What if I chose to simply get married before I finished my education? I believe all these questions and concerns were partly to blame for my father's being strict and too ambitious about academic excellence. Evidently, I was faced with two realms of scrutiny. What was the community talking at the end of each semester? Everyone loved to talk about their children's performance. Osteen (2005) writes:

When you go through disappointments in life and we all do or when you face a setback and it looks as though one of your dreams has died, keep believing. When it looks dark and dreary and you don't see any way out, remind yourself that ...no obstacle will be too high, no situation too difficult. The darkest battle, the darkest storm will always give way to the brightest sunrise. Keep pressing forward (p.136-137).

I needed to hear these words, but instead I engraved myself in my own disappointment and the feeling of fear regarding my performance.

Now as a parent, I am aware that showing compassion to a child that has been wounded is rewarding because love is vital in everyone's life. Children especially are exceptionally sensitive-what they need is genuine attention from caring parents! Children depend on their parents or care givers during the most difficult times and they need to feel that strength. When there is outside strength, there also develops an inner strength for the child to remain focused. At last, I got that with the support and loving hand from my parents. They did not despair, but instead gave me the hope to remain positive and focused on my studies.

Struggles with School

At age sixteen I entered grade seven. One may wonder how a sixteen-year-old girl could only be in grade seven. I only picked up normal schooling after leaving my aunt's place when I was already eleven years old. In developed countries, I should have been in grade eleven. When I returned to my parents, I started grade two. To my admiration, my first semester at this school under the care of my parents was the determining factor of my present day career.

I felt the potential to succeed. My parents were extremely happy to see their little girl change from being shy to being a happy girl who demonstrated she had a promising future! As a parent, I have come to understand the difference between children who grow up without parents and the challenges a child experiences trying to determine his/her identity. I found my identity around my parents and this caused my study habits to change for the better.

In this new environment, I found complete confidence and having everything needed to realize what I needed to succeed because, my parents were around to support me whatever the struggles. As Gray (1999) points out, "With this positive attitude of personal success, there is no reason or need to hold on to blaming others" (p.219). I did not have the desire or feeling or memories of what had happened to me at my aunt's. My next five years in this new environment/ school, were of ambitions to join university; I told myself. When you hold on to your ambitions, do not let anyone take it away from you. I walked 10 kilometers back and forth to school, Monday to Friday.

With all these experiences of childhood struggles and now a mother, I have come to understand that when a child is placed in a good caring environment, there is a feeling of security that leads to positive aspirations. I do not think that there was anything different from the teachings that I had in my early life, the system was the same! It was only the environment with parental love and care that I missed at my aunt's place, which led to my inability to perform well in class.

While growing up, there were no hot lunches as many children in the Western culture enjoy. We used to wake up in the morning sometimes without breakfast; we went to school, and spent the whole day without eating. We only had one meal, dinner. That was my typical day! This led to some health problems, such as ulcers. It is well documented that three essentials for life and a well-balanced mind in a child are: breakfast, lunch and dinner, which in most cases I did not get!

Yet, even when I went through these ordeals, my family was considered one of the well to do in the community, but I could go to school on an empty stomach! Other children from other families were going through the same trend. So this looked normal at the time. I still found this kind of life style much better than where I spent my three years without my parents. Although there were many times when I stayed at school on an empty stomach in my new environment, I still felt at peace because I got a sense of being loved and valued by my parents and other family members.

Grade seven was the entry level that determined whether one would make it to high school or some college education. In this grade entry, I had also reached maturity age where I needed a boyfriend. If it were like in the current situation of my parenthood, telephones and texting would consistently be off the hook. But this was not the case. I remained focused on high school entry despite my struggles.

In grade 7 I had a boyfriend, who is now my husband. This boyfriend did not distract me from my focus. We communicated quite frequently while he was also a student in college far from where I lived. As we started our relationship, we both agreed to wait for each other until when ready to have a family. "When you always keep your promises, simply by giving your word you will draw in the power to manifest your word…each time you succeed in keeping a promise, you will grow in the power to keep your word"(Gray, 1999: p.240). It took us six and a half more years before we finally got married after we had both finished with school.

The disillusion and path change toward my dream

Before being admitted to a tertiary institution in Uganda in the late 1970s, three exams had to be passed: Mathematics, English and Social Studies. My first attempt to do this entry exam was disastrous. Mathematics became a barrier to achieving my academic aspirations. My parents did not want me to go to a public school due to the negative reports that they heard about such institutions. They preferred that I go to a boarding school, which in most cases was government sponsored and in the city. Unfortunately, I believed I would never pass grade 7 because, mathematics was totally difficult for me.

This was a "false prophesy." Joseph Mensah (2002) writes, "until recently many were those who took as gospel truth the view that women were not as smart or as good in mathematics and science as men" (p.196). When I failed the second time, I became convinced that this was the end of my aspiration. Self-pity crept in. It was so demoralizing that I went back to the words I kept in my recycled mind bin, "I am a failure." This diminished my self-motivation. My stomach ulcers got worse. I did not want to go to a public school, but unfortunately that was what my grade average qualified me for.

Gray (1999) writes:

One of the big problems with self-pity is that we not only miss opportunities for more, but we reject them as well. As if to justify our misery, we stay there. We believe that we have missed out, and nothing can make up for it. We feel sorry for ourselves, and we do not want anything to change that (253).

Self-pity, shame and disappointment were almost throwing me into a panic! Thankfully, my father remained hopeful and continued to encourage me in my academic aspirations. The cultural characteristics of a successful girl/daughter pressured me severely. My broken and unfulfilled dream of not going to university caused me great pain. But "pain can be used to serve a purpose. It will do work in our lives to make us bitter or better. The choice is ours" (Jaynes, 2004: p.159). It was up to me to decide whether I keep my academic dream or drop it and get married to my fiancé who was waiting for me. In my case, the seemingly shattered dream stirred my appetite "for a higher purpose or a higher calling or a higher love or a higher trust" (ibid).

Finally, after the third attempt, I got admission to college. Mathematics was still the lowest score out of the three required subjects, but what I learnt through my struggles with grade seven was to choose the alternative. I realized that my dream of finishing grade seven and going to high school, then university, was no longer real. I had to take the short cut from grade seven to a teacher training college instead of high school. This was extremely painful and demoralizing for me. While some other people don't care that much about academic success, there are those who feel very low and inferior as though they are failures in every aspect of life if they do not do well in school.

What I did not understand was that there is always hope if one is still alive. People who continued to give me hope were my parents. They knew what they had committed themselves to, investing in their daughter's education! Thanks to God and my parents who never let me burry my dream; a dream to come with even more potential for fruition. My new desire was to get a degree in education if this is what it took to make me a "woman of status."

That childhood determination has not only become a stepping stool for my current educational achievement and social mobility, but has also been a means to understand the different populations that I have worked with over the years since I came to Canada. Even though I chose the short-cut of going to a teachers college, my parents were happy because they had wanted me to be a teacher after all. I have listened empathetically and attentively to young adults with all sorts of challenges, young women and couples that have had their own shares of life as a result of one or more of what I have also experienced.

I look back and realize that whatever we wish for our children, if we walk with them, they will achieve it if they are willing to be supported. Even though I changed career in my adult years, I still find myself teaching my children, and talking as a teacher to the women with whom I have shared my experience in this book. Teaching remains my profession even though I am now a social worker by profession! Through these experiences, I have also learnt some lessons, especially the lessons of loving those who hurt. I have learnt to be a listener and a supporter for my children when they make decisions regarding their future, without being judgmental. I have learnt to stand with them without them feeling a sense of abandonment.

Where possible, I have tried to guide them if they are willing to take my advice, without imposing my own opinion on them. It has been a common practice for me in my social work practice to ensure that I use the listening principle to ensure my clientele does not feel worthless. To help them translate their pains for love; their disruption for contentment; and isolation for inclusion is vital in my professional work. One may ask, when does love become love? When love stands challenges, betrayal, and lack of trust or unfaithfulness? Stanley explains love as:

> Love has no season-it is all seasons. I believe there is no greater power to change the hurting people's climate than extending a loving hand to them. Love can be characterized into seven traits: Kindness-discovering the joy of treating others as persons of worth; patience-accepting the imperfections of others; forgiveness-finding freedom from the grip of anger; courtesy-treating others as friends; humility-stepping down so someone else can step up; generosity- offering time, abilities, and money to help others; honesty-speaking the truth in love (Stanley, 2009: p. 14)

These are qualities that we all need to develop when we meet people who do not look like ourselves. Love is the most powerful tool that can heal wounds where there have been painful experiences. In my situation, love from my parents made me survive my school years and it is love that I believe can give those who have given up on their ambitions to get a second chance in life. Although I have not yet been perfected in my love practice with people I work with, love has become my instrument in my daily practice in my interactions with people. Gary Chapman (2009), points out that, "Love is the most powerful weapon in the world for good. I am convinced that love not only stands a chance in the contemporary world; it is, in fact, our only chance of survival" (p.15).

Based on my own lived experiences, I agree with Chapman. It can be difficult to talk above difficult childhood memories, especially when they have been carried into adulthood. But it is not impossible. Adebaye (2008) declares the power inherent in renaming our ugly past-salvaging what was good and discarding the rest. He writes:

> Whatever has been created on earth ought to have a name. Situations and circumstances have names. Any unpleasant

situation can be renamed. Renaming a thing or an event can be done effectively or ineffectively. It is effective when pronouncement is done with the power (of people who believe in you)…any name you have been given capable of limiting or negating your destiny must be dropped for excellence (p.51).

Osteen agrees. He writes:

Words that are spoken positively will always have an effect on someone's life. Equally important are the words that have been spoken negatively into someone's life. Let these words resonate in your ears and eyes until you see daylight. It will for sure come if you can only get a different perspective on how life should be looked at-positive attitude!! You may not realize it, but it is extremely selfish to be dwelling on your problems, always thinking about what you want or need and hardly noticing the many needs of others all around you. One of the best things you can do if you're having a problem is to help solve somebody else's problem. If you want your {ambitions} to come to pass, help someone else fulfill his or her dreams (Osteen, 2005: pp. 253-4).

Journey with my husband and dreams of a life of status

"I wanted to be a bride and a mother, but most of all have someone who cherished me" (Jaynes, 2004: p. 37). "My princess dream started very young. Like most little girls, I played dress-up, putting on long dresses and high-heeled shoes. My house was my castle, and I dreamed of being rescued by a handsome prince who would love me and take away all my hurts" (Jaynes, 2004: p. 72).

Words that we say usually inspire us to reach the goals that we set before us and the same words motivate us to reach our potential. The words of a young girl came to pass as I had prophesied in my childhood life, to get married and be a woman who would be loved and respected. I had the dream of being a "woman of status", and marrying a man of my dreams with certain qualities and personalities, a man with whom I would find true love! These dreams seemed to have some significance because they inspired me to work harder in every aspect, stay focused especially in my academic aspirations. I got married to my sweetheart in 1981 after waiting over 6 years for him. One year before we got married, my husband got involved in politics and I became a "woman of status" by virtue of being a wife of a Member of Parliament!

In my new status of "wife of a Member of Parliament", I also engaged myself in community development work through Uganda Young Women's Christian Association (YWCA). The association encourages women to participate in a model literacy and development project sponsored by Pro Literacy's partner, the *YWCA of Uganda*. Using locally developed materials in the native language, participants gain the skills and confidence to initiate efforts for solving problems related to food production, health, housing, environmental conservation, parenting, and income generation.

I worked as a community social worker even though I did not have the professional training of being a social worker! In these roles, I had the opportunity to go for training through workshops, which equipped me with the knowledge about community social work. These trainings enhanced my fight for human rights of rural women who were poor. It also stimulated me to support the cause of what YWCA promoted, enhancing the lives of those who were out of reach by the local governments, hence supplying the women with seeds for their subsistence farming.

As I passionately got engaged with this group of women, I chose to do what I loved most and decided to divide my work. I taught the school kids for three days and two days for work in the community with women in my husband's constituency. Each day that passed by, I became more deeply and passionately involved working with these rural women. However, it was not an easy task juggling these responsibilities while focusing on my duties as a wife to the area's Member of Parliament. Most importantly, I found joy in helping these women, making a difference in their welfare, and chose to resign from teaching. After resigning from teaching, I knew that these women needed my total support. Some of them were widows as a result of diseases and wars.

As I look back at how the women expressed themselves, it is clear to me that there were signs of trauma experienced as a result of running family responsibilities single handedly. Some were in situations where their deceased husbands had left them with children numbering between four and seven under undesirable living conditions. Some of the children slept on empty stomachs; and some women had been abused by the relatives of their husbands who confiscated their properties.

At the time when I worked with these women, I was not knowledgeable about trauma. After immigrating to Canada and the many publications that I have read about it, I now realize these women had effects of trauma resulting from multiple losses experienced. Many of the women explained to me about the constant headaches, the lack of sleep and in most cases unexplained body aches, which I now understand as somatization. Some of these explanations did not make any sense or have any meaning to me before I got interested in the mental health of women.

At least most of the women that came to my presentations had gone through some kind of emotional trauma after losing their husbands. Cultural systems, require that the wealth of the deceased husband is left to the brother of the deceased man, with anticipation that the brother takes over the family and looks after the deceased man's children. Such arrangements often left the woman in a financial crisis. As a result, many families experienced a very steep reduction in the standard of living.

It is obvious that when you love what you do, you will always learn the skills or find the mechanism to do your best, even though you may not have the training to do the job. Having worked with people who suffer from war trauma, I have realized that I was dealing with traumatized women that needed healing. With my naivety, I tried to convince these women to remain positive, even though in some instances it was not easy to simply forget about their pain while living a poor life. Despite my lack of professional training in the area of counseling, using a holistic approach, I was there to plant a seed of hope in their hearts and inspire them about positive thinking. It was a terrible hardship for them because no matter what we shared in a group, the pain of being poor could not go away. The trauma pain does not go away; it has to be worked through.

During the 1960s up until the mid-1990s, poverty, and lack of formal land ownership, made loans difficult to access in Uganda, hence limiting agricultural improvements and other economic alternatives (Ellis, Manuel & Blackden, 2006; Tamale, 2001; Tripp, 2004). In this framework the development of micro-credit (Kirimba) groups that make small sums available on a rotating basis, had profound impacts on improving both the economic and social status of women.

The rural women I worked with, gardening became our social support network and a source of generating macro ideas. There was empowerment in this kind of arrangement, where groups of ten women had a small plot/garden and planted tomatoes and cabbages. Herman (1997) clearly highlights the benefit of a group support network for people who have gone through trauma. She states that "Groups have proved invaluable for survivors of extreme situations, including combat, rape, political persecution, battering, and childhood abuse… [poor and isolated women repeatedly said that] their solace was in simply being present with others who have endured similar ordeal" (p.214).

In this community, these women had felt so alienated by their experience of being widows and poor. As I worked with them, a bond formed between them and myself. There were times when we held group discussions where women opened up about their personal experiences. I was no longer viewed as their member of parliament's wife or "woman of status", but as one who belonged to them and shared with them their pain. Again, Herman's findings about traumatized individuals provide additional insight. She writes:

Traumatized people feel so alienated by their experience. Such groups afford a degree of support and understanding that is simply not available in the survivor's ordinary social environment. They encounter with others who have undergone similar trails, and dissolve feelings of isolation, shame, and stigma (p.215).

In the African context, intimacy is not only discussing things; but also doing things together as a group of women, while laughing and fully engaged in productive activities that bring food to the table. Bringing hoes and seeds to the women resulted in a sense of voicing their concerns, which would otherwise not be shared if such a group were not established. I was not the woman of "status", but someone who was passionately busy recruiting and bringing women together for a common cause, fighting poverty through gardening. As a result, this brought a nutrition program to the community of Rwentutu, in my husband's constituency. Women developed cohesion and intimacy that they extended to others who were isolated, thus making themselves participants rather than mere observers. I was able to put down my mesmerizing notion of a "woman of status" while traveling and doing community work. I felt happy doing what brought change in the lives of these community women. Omartian (2004) points out that:

The proof of our sincerity is in the doing, not just the knowing. It's one thing to make a list of do's and don'ts, but it's quite another to have a heart for [those who are suffering] and a soul that longs to live them out (p.54).

When Parliament was in recess, my husband would come with me to deliver hoes, seeds and other essential materials that supported women in their gardening. It was evident that when women saw their Member of Parliament and myself deliver the gardening items/tools, there was a feeling of joy and excitement. Most of these women lived without hope after broken dreams, which needed someone to rebuild. Collaboratively we all worked together to try and meet these dreams on a small-scale basis.

I had the joy and privileges that these women did not. My rationale for being part of the community development program through YWCA was to make women and children's faces shine with smiles and bring hope to their shattered dreams, despite the odds they consistently faced, poverty. The momentum that the YWCA gathered for poor women in the country fueled a wave of rural women wanting to join this program.

What Jaynes (2004) writes about a brighter future is what I was aiming at. She states, "For the first time in [these women's] life, the sun shone brighter, [their] eyes danced with excitement and joy" (p.46). Given the domestic routines, and expenses of living in the African community/family, keeping a home and raising children or nurturing a community of any kind can be painful, especially where the only source of income is by subsistence farming. In this part of the world, there are to this day some places that are faced with draught, and/or with mudslides. The odds outweigh the benefits especially if there is no other source of income.

For the women who were widowed, their only option was to continue farming the land if given the opportunity by their husbands' clans to keep the land. Their hope was in their children's success in school if they had the means to educate them. Mensah (2002) clearly points out:

While men have greater socio-economic and political power than women across the globe, this power imbalance is far more entrenched in Africa. Consequently, in most African families it is only the men who have the resources and the power to embark on such [opportunities of gaining fame and wealth because they have the capacity of occupational background] (p.117).

Growing up in Africa and being a "woman of status" by virtue of being a wife of the Member of Parliament, I did not experience the same restrictions as other women. This gave me the privilege to reach out to them and be part of their grass roots network. In the 1970s and 80s, patriarchy was still dominant in many parts of Africa. Mensah (2002) confirms this by pointing out that "...African men would still gain access to [resources] than their female counterparts.

This law may not apply in many advanced societies now, but it is still relevant in the African context due to the extreme patriarchy in African culture" (Ibid). Excitingly, during my visit to the community, there were discussions of education for their children, poverty and self-reliance. Gradually as the women became aware of my presence as a wife of their MP, they started coming to check me out. The word spread out that I was approachable and there was value in meeting me and planning together what they needed for their community.

Helping women fighting poverty

I begin this section with these words of hope that have helped and inspired me in my work:

> Dear God, as I reaffirm my commitment to reach out to the poor, the women and children around me, I ask you to give me the words to help them sort through their emotional feelings. Let them know how really special and loved they are; how good life really is when faced with courage and support from others. Let hope be the attitude for their tomorrows. I ask you to help me be the role model women and children require. May my voice speak the words they need to hear? Let me be able to support them to provide them solace. God, these are the gifts that instill hope (words adopted from Marta, S.Y.'s book, 2003: pp. 290).

Women and children experience chronic hunger because they cannot produce enough food or do not earn enough to buy the food they need. It is obvious that the vast majority of these poor and hungry women in our world work very hard to provide for themselves and their families. Hunger and poverty are intertwined and mutually reinforcing conditions. When women couldn't sell their food crops such as maize, cassava or potatoes for a better price, they couldn't afford to feed their families either. At the time it was even harder for single mothers and widows to sustain their families on a single income. In worst cases, if the head of the family was deceased, his property was taken over by the next of kin, his brother, not the wife because of fear that the widow would get married to another man who is not a relative, and then the wealth of the deceased would go to the next man.

In other cases, a deceased man's brother was asked to look after his brother's property, which included the widow and her children. Such arrangements were for the protection of the deceased person's property. With this cultural norm, the widow was virtually left with nothing, but only to depend on the person responsible for the family. This is demonstrated in one woman's experience who explains the situation in the community where she grew up.

> I am fully responsible for my children. I have to take care of their education, I have to discipline them, and I have to take care of them in all the possible ways I can until they become mature" (interview by Wasik, 2006).

In the African culture, a lot of emphasis is placed on extended family values such as when the widow is asked to be under the guidance of the deceased's brother, the widow is obliged to accept such an arrangement. Generally, polygamy is a common practice in many parts of Africa. If the brother is able to take care of his deceased brother's responsibilities and property, which means having multiple wives and children on top of what he already has. In some instances though, the brother may simply not accept the added responsibility. If the widow was a stay home wife with no education, this then becomes an added burden to her, because the property would have to be transferred to another family member. I have to admit that in some parts of Africa, things are changing because of education, especially for girls who get married when already academically advanced. Another woman puts it this way:

> In our culture, the father is the chief in the family. If he dies, the whole family suffers because the wife has not been used to supporting the family" (interview by Wasik, 2006).

The findings of Masinda and Kambere (2008) collaborate with what the woman has identified as the norm in the African cultures. They contend:

Many family structures are patriarchal with a prominent value devoted to the father. When a family member dies, the orphans are taken care of by family members, mostly uncles and aunts if big brothers or big sisters do not have the capacity to take over the responsibility (p.13).

In order for me to bring meaningful purpose to the women in the rural area of Rwentutu in Kasese, it was important to address the issue of hunger and poverty; emphasizing sustainable approaches to economic development, that empower poor people, especially women. Most importantly, the support systems at community level that focused only on what the women needed and felt would most benefit their families and the community as a whole.

A value for their culture upholds that, *"we have to share what we have with our neighbor who is our brother"*. This kind of approach has sustained some of these cultures and enabled them to thrive. It is also reflected in Osteen's (2005) writing where he states:

You must learn to be a giver and not a taker. Quit trying to figure out what everybody can do for you, and start trying to figure out what you can do for somebody else. We were not made to function as self-involved people, thinking only of ourselves…and you will never be truly fulfilled as a human being until you learn the simple secret of how to give your life away" (ps.253-4).

In these communities, many people rely heavily on the extended family. The "nuclear family" has very little significance for them. When we started working on the poor women's programs, they did not only benefit the individual family, but the community as a whole. Women shared the problems and the bounty. This is a cultural norm, collectivity and hospitality which the women were used to. For example when the team I worked with from YWCA went to deliver gardening tools and seeds, the whole community got together to welcome us. Men who were not part of the program also came to be part of the celebration. There was entertainment and sharing with us the little food they had because there was something to celebrate about, seeds, that would eventually multiply and feed the whole community. In many of the African cultures, eating together is part of their celebration. It is also an aspect of honor and appreciation.

The YWCA's mission was to work with community workers, to train and educate them about nutrition. It was important for me to be part of this eradication of poverty in my community and the entire district. In our meetings with the executives of YWCA, our slogan was that we must support the efforts of poor people to produce enough food to feed their families. It was also important to empower women to enable them to get opportunities of having decent meals for their school age children. Education and training for the women to earn enough to buy the food they needed was vital in all aspects. In the second year of working with YWCA (1985), the association had started supplying bicycles to support community workers to reach their respective areas of work. I was given a bicycle like any other worker. I did not need a bicycle because I had the means to travel to the community. I chose to give my bicycle to one of the volunteers with whom I worked to help him reach places that I was not able to visit in a timely manner.

Coincidentally, during this process many women who were based in Rwentutu developed a lot of ideas to do other developmental projects. The area where I worked with these women was not close to any government hospital. Children were dying of Malaria due to lack of medical facilities in the area. During our gatherings, women decided that with the help of YWCA, a clinic be opened in the area where women could access medical services and supplies. One of the husbands (I will call him Mark) in the community had a grass thatched building with about seven rooms, which women requested that he allows them to use as a clinic. The man was kind enough to release it to the women because, he had seen the potential this project would bring to the community as a whole.

This man had envisioned how pregnant women would be better served, given the high mortality rate in the community. The big heart Mark had showed best practices for serving the poor in his community. It further revealed areas for improving services to the families and building respectful relationships between communities and YWCA. Mark had a big dream that would save many lives, especially the poor and vulnerable whose dreams had been shattered by natural disasters. As Jaynes (2004) points out "Some dreams are shattered by what has happened to us and some dreams are shattered because of what has happened through us-the choice we have made" (p.175). Mark's passion to help others was revived by someone coming to the community where he lived. Mark felt that when women are helped, the whole community benefits.

Ideas were developed that demonstrated a holistic and culturally sensitive practice cognizant to the women's indigenous capacities, rooted in their desire to secure a better future for their children, who could only get education if these mothers became part of the big picture. Subsequently the work that we did with parents focused on helping them to improve their ability to manage and cope with stress, and empowering them to realize and use the skills they had without any formal education. I was particularly touched by how some women expressed their gratitude to me for being involved in their activities, and sharing their wish that "I want my daughter to be like you (Edith) when she finishes her school."

In most cases, these compliments were accompanied by feelings of guilt because, I did not want their daughters to go through the struggles that I had, especially during my school time! Nonetheless, I found that my feelings were quite normal given that everyone wants a successful life without any struggles. When we hear of people who have made it, it is usually not without struggles. I recall feeling a sense of relief and joy as I sat with these women and shared their experiences and what they wanted to accomplish through the YWCA program.

These women's words were inspiring, liberating and greatly influenced my current work with immigrant and refugee women who come from war torn countries. I saw the determination they had, especially those with the inspirations of wanting their children to go to school, a dream that most families had for their children.

Life of status tested in prison

The government's fall in 1986 was the beginning of a new path to challenges and disappointment. My husband was arrested and put in prison as a former politician. This brought a new focus to new things. It was a time to taste the bitterness of life. Even if I had the desire to visit some of the women that I had developed connections with, I now felt isolation. These political changes have been the norm in African societies. Specifically in my case the situation was even much more complicated given that after the fall of the Uganda People's Congress (UPC) government on 27th July 1985 there was yet another government takeover by rebels on 26th July, 1986. When the government that one supported or associated with falls, many people become victims of scorn, harassment and in most cases lose privileges and property. In my case, I lost at least most of the property that I had during the fall of the first government. What I did not know while working with the rural women was that soon, I was going to experience the very poverty level they were going through. Indeed, it was even worse. I became like them within a short time.

I was poor and had nothing to feed my two young kids. Sometimes we slept on empty stomachs. Where possible I went to the neighbors to beg for food. It was very embarrassing, but I remained hopeful that one day, this situation would end. My husband was now in the Uganda maximum security prison where most of the previous regime politicians were locked up. It took me a twelve hours' train ride to go and visit him. It was costly and I needed enough resources to support the two children and then a husband in prison. I sold most of the valuables that we had, such as cars and other household essentials. He was in prison for 18 months. For the rest of the time he was in prison, I was sick with unexplained aches.

The doctors I visited could not identify any sickness. I was very depressed and had constant heart palpitations. I developed panic attacks each time I heard a loud bang or something falling off the wall. I would tremble from head to foot. My head would pound so hard and fast. I was sure it would jump right out of my chest. I would break out with a cold sweat, and sometimes sob uncontrollably. As I look back and after studying the effects of war, I realize that I was suffering some effects of trauma! In 1987, my husband was released by the high court after government failed to produce evidence against him. Given that it was a politically motivated arrest, it was prudent for him not stay in case of a re-arrest. He took advantage of his bail and immediately escaped into exile, in the nearby country of the Democratic Republic of Congo (then called Zaire). I followed him with one child a year later, but without our older son due to the difficult circumstances. He stayed behind with our family. We lived in Congo for five years.

Although I had lost the public status, there were positive aspects to celebrate. I had planted a seed in these women and was hopeful one day the seed would be revived. I maintained such a strong conviction that one day and soon, we would come back and continue with the work that we had just started. It came to pass as I had wished, but not as soon as I had expected. It came back twenty years later after both my husband and I had been released from the anger and bitterness we had harbored toward the people we felt we had served faithfully, but eventually betrayed us. Amazingly, in Rwentutu community, there is now an elementary school, and a women's micro-finance lending project, a medical health clinic for kids; which are a testimony to the importance of "never giving up on your dream!"

The road to exile

July 27, 1985 was like any other day. The beautiful sky over Kasese, a small town in Western Uganda bordering The Democratic Republic of Congo was cloudless and blue. My husband went to work to perform his usual parliamentary duties. A young and energetic MP who was responsible for his constituency duties when the late Dr. Milton Obote was president. I was scheduled to go to a cousin's wedding with a group of friends in Bwera, a town close to the border of Uganda and the Democratic Republic of Congo not far from where my husband was working. At the time, I was pregnant with our second son. Our firstborn was staying with a baby sitter[house girl].

Before we arrived at our destination, we were stopped by a group of confused and disgruntled people standing by the roadside at a local market, 5 kilometers from the border. I recognized some of them as supporters of the Uganda People's Congress, the government's ruling party. Among the crowds were a few relatives who informed us that the government of Uganda had just been overthrown. I simply smiled as one cousin delivered the news to me while she was leaning to the window of the car where I was seated. I could hardly believe what I was hearing because the magnitude of what I had just been told was lost on me. My cousin was on the other hand confused by the demeanor that I portrayed, by simply behaving naively as though I had not heard her deliver the news to me. Her response to this behavior was "you even have the audacity to smile?"

We were advised not to proceed for the wedding ceremony, but to retreat and/or flee for our lives. We chose to go back to Kasese and be with the family members. As we drove back to Kasese, we passed groups of people running for their lives. Cars were carrying people going toward the border of the Congo; we were the only car on the road headed back to Kasese. It was chaotic all around but we simply had to get back to our loved ones. As we drove, the radio filled us in about what had just happened in our country.

On the radio, we heard those who had overthrown the Obote government talk words of threats like "we shall leave no stone unturned." They also reported how few of the ministers that worked in the Obote government had been arrested as they tried to escape to the neighboring Kenya. There were also some assurances from the captures that people should remain calm and that the situation will soon be under control. These mixed messages were not of any hope to us who were in the fallen regime. Throughout the approximately 45 minute ride, except for the news broadcasts, there was silence in the car. Each of us was silently calculating the possibility, if not the risk, of making it back, safely to Kasese.

When we finally arrived, the whole town seemed totally deserted except for military personnel. There were no civilians to be seen anywhere but only army vehicles carrying soldiers and heavy artillery everywhere. I had no idea where, or if, I would find my husband and eldest son whom I had left with the baby sitter. In third world countries when governments are overthrown, it is commonplace to round up all the politicians of the deposed government and throw them in jail. I feared the worst for my husband. When I arrived at my home, I found that it had already been evacuated. A few boxes packed with household items lay scattered around.

I began to search the house, but only to find no sign of anyone in the house. I started panicking fearing for the worst. I started calling while opening every room, but with nobody to respond. The people whom I had come with from the wedding had gone their ways. I started sweating. All rooms were evacuated. I went to the fridge to see if my baby's food was still there or if my house girl had done some cooking.

But I only found the fridge intact with all the food still there as I had left it the previous night. My heart started pounding. The feeling was so intense fearing for the worst for my son and my husband. In the bedroom, there was no sign of even a note from my husband to tell me where he might have gone with the baby. The fear of whether my husband was able to make it from the office to the house was so high. The sad thing is that I was a lone in the house. There was no one to ask about anything. This ordeal took me about twenty minutes. But this was like a day's search. Even though I was pregnant, I had no desire to eat, not even to get food from the fridge as I headed out to check with my neighbors.

Having searched the entire house, I found myself at a neighbor's house where, to my great relief, I discovered my husband and son hiding with our maid. This neighbor's house was up the hill where it was easy for anyone to see an enemy who might want to take a search. It was also an easy route for escape to the mountains. Besides, the neighbor was my maid's relative and thus the most likely place to expect my husband and maid to have taken refuge.

Although the time driving and searching for my family seemed to pass by so slowly, it all happened so fast. Within hours, my life as a young MP's wife and my dream of a life of status had been shattered. Prior to the coup d'état, my life had been that of a public figure. I did public speaking engagements; I was involved in women and community program activities, as well as an elementary school teacher. Then, in the span of just a few hours, I began to experience the horror of what happens when a government is violently overthrown. Everything around us showed no sign of hope for us to survive in this new government. We were isolated from what used to be our social cluster which feared to be called associates. We had two personal cars. One day I saw my driver come home without my car, but barefooted; he looked exhausted as he approached the house, but only to deliver the message that the car had been hijacked by the army men as he was on his way to town to buy groceries. I was pregnant and became speechless as he delivered the news. I started panicking about what the future was going to hold for us with this kind of intimidation.

First of all, we were not criminals that deserved even personal property to be hijacked. This left me with no transport to carry my personal effects such as furniture, and beds to a place of safety. I developed such hatred and fear for anyone associated with the new government. Secondly, the second car was too small and it was not safe to dare put it on the road to carry any items due to the tension around us.

Fear creeped in, as the situation became increasingly unfriendly for us. The scorning, laughing from the population around us, and the talking was a common phenomenon as my son and I passed people who were anti previous regime. It was dreadful for us to go to church; there was isolation and lack of trust from anyone, especially those who were associated with the new regime. The whole environment was full of army vehicles patrolling with army men carrying their artilleries.

Three months after the coup, I had my second born. The condition remained hostile for a young mother. The means of survival to feed two little kids was difficult as both my husband and I were without jobs. We depended on the little savings that we had, and also on the dry foods that our parents sent us. Ten months after the coup, the army insisted on occupying our house and I was forced to get out. Gracefully, we were helped by one friend who allowed us to take our personal items to his one-bedroom suite.

As we were given only few hours to be out of the house, some of the neighbors came and helped us carry the mattresses, beds, kitchen stuff, and children's items to this one bedroom suite. At this time, the whole neighborhood was alarmed as the events unfolded. Some good Samaritans came and helped to carry these items on their heads to the new location, which was about a block away. Unfortunately, at the time, technology was not advanced as to communicate with our family members for help, especially to carry some light items such as clothes, dishes and beddings to the village. After being evicted from our house, we became even more isolated because no one wanted to be associated with us.

Life did not get any better after the move from the previous location. I scrambled in a small house with my two children and my maid when these supporters of the new regime came and surrounded the building, singing and rejoicing. My husband was not a criminal, just a victim of the fallen government. I was psychologically traumatized and fearful as the celebrations continued throughout the district. I did not know what was going to unfold for me and my family, but I tried to maintain a positive attitude, thinking that this would not be continuous chaos. I thought it might last for a month or two then things would get back to business as usual. Alas, that was not to be. Rather, it proved to be a long journey of many winding roads.

Our family status and class changed virtually overnight. I began to learn what it was like to be displaced. The country continued to be in an uproar, especially throughout the various districts. My husband and his colleagues were forced into hiding, and I was left to support my little family with virtually no income. My two little children hungered for a nutritious meal which their mother could not afford. We sometimes slept on empty stomachs. There were times when I went to the neighbor's house to ask for food to give my children.

With every day that passed, the situation grew worse. I longed for the misery to end, but it went on. The situation worsened for my family. We started receiving threatening messages of wanting to round up previous politicians, and of course my husband was a target. He remained in hiding, and I also stayed with my two children and our housemaid. There were lots of scorning, spitting at me by supporters of the new regime as I passed by. It appeared as though I was imprisoned within my own surrounding, where reaching out to my relatives for social support was impossible. I lived a life of solitude with only the Bishop's wife coming to visit me, to pray and encourage me throughout this ordeal.

As the harassment continued, I took refuge at our Bishop's house where I stayed for few days before I could decide to go back in the village to live with my parents. The feeling of looking at people who looked at me as a destitute was very humiliating. The only best solution was for me to move from this part of the town and go back into the village to live with my parents. The bishop drove me to my parents' house, but was stopped at a roadblock by the militia half-way to our destination. He was interrogated by two angry militia; he was asked who I was and where he was taking me. Before he could complete the sentence of explaining to them who I was and where he was taking me, he was slapped in the face.

The scenario looked as though I was in a dream. My eyes could not believe what I saw happen to my bishop. The militia started searching the car; my boy, the first born started crying; the bishop's two teenage daughters who had also accompanied us remained calm as they saw their father being humiliated. To me, it felt like the world had collapsed on us, not sure whether we were going to be short at or thrown into the bushes. I expected the worse. I was impacted emotionally and physically by what had happened to the Bishop.

The bishop went through all this for just having carried me to safety. He was told to go back to town. This incident and the additional army roadblocks that had been set up all over the district made it impossible for me to get around, especially since the current government was rounding up former political leaders. With this new change in government, I was faced with the challenge of fitting into the community without being identified as 'the former MP's wife,' an identity not pleasant to wear among the local people.

It took hard work on my part to establish a social network that would accept me. Most of my associates had deserted me! It seemed like a bad dream, but it was real. There was no more luxurious life of driving around for women's meetings or social gatherings. Miraculously, in spite of this incident and the mental and emotional turmoil that came with it, God gave me the grace to develop an attitude of looking at life positively despite what I was going through. I learned to accept the adversity with gratitude.

As weeks tuned into months, my confusion and mental turmoil increased. Many politicians were rounded up and imprisoned. Although there were still fears that my husband could be a victim, we did our best to maintain a positive attitude. We decided to try to live like any person in the district and accept the change that had occurred, despite all the rumors that were circulating around about political leaders from the previous regime. People were saying all sorts of things, such as "you used to sing no change, now the change has come for you and you are now living like us", yet another even said, "the previous regime was the worst I have ever lived in". Other talks were oh she felt her husband would permanently be called "honorable", so how is she going to identify her husband? Such scornful talking remained for a long time.

We remained with a positive mindset. What we thought and felt was ideal for us was to start our own primary school because, both of us had been professional teachers before our political life. To embark on this new venture, we chose to sell some of our valuables in order to get finances to start this formidable task. I had a grade two teaching certificate. I decided to go for grade three teaching upgrade, while my husband stayed at home working on the construction of the school. At the time, the situation was not yet safe for us to start such a venture.

We hoped nothing would disrupt this plan. Within one week into my upgrading program, I got news that my husband had been arrested. I had to discontinue the program and return home to take care of our two little boys. Since my husband had committed no crime, I thought he would be released following routine questioning, I was wrong, that arrest turned into an 18 months incarceration in Luzira, Uganda's Maximum Prison.

He was in this prison with many other politicians, and when the state could not produce enough evidence to build up a case against him, he was released by the high court. On hearing rumors of another arrest, we decided that he take refuge in neighboring Democratic republic of Congo, as mentioned earlier. The journey for me remained of more scorn, questioning, sickness and isolation. Some of our relatives were put in prison under suspicion that they helped my husband escape. The urge to have my husband back mounted even higher than what we had experienced immediately after the coup d'état.

With time, no one wanted to be associated with me. Each day that went by, there were rumors that I would be arrested for interrogation about my husband's whereabouts. I decided to follow him to the Democratic Republic of Congo.

I made my trip secretly; I did not even tell my parents. Instead, I connected with another colleague, a wife of a former MP from the same district whose husband had also been imprisoned in the same prison as my husband. Both of us decided to cross over to follow our husbands. I did not know the local DRC language; neither did my friend. Neither of us was familiar with either the local language (Swahili) or French. When we crossed the border, we had to make alliances with some market vendors who came to Uganda for business in order for them to help us cross over into Congo.

We had to arrange this journey secretly for the local people not to know about it, and so as to avoid a similar situation like one when I traveled with the Bishop. I left everything behind, including a three year old son. I took refuge with the younger one, my two year old boy. The experience of relocating from all that had been familiar to me left me tormented, in strange surroundings, and hungry. I was left with the appearance of someone who had never eaten a decent meal, but I was determined to face these new challenges in a new environment where no one knew anything about my previous life. It was these experiences that caused me to step back and question whether the values I had upheld as "good" more closely modeled my culture or made my self-image? Indeed, my self-image was being severely tested.

In this new environment I needed to start developing a new social life, values, and norms. I did not know the language of the country, neither did I know the culture. I did not even know where I could go and buy the essential commodities for our daily use, things like charcoal, cooking oil, fufu [flour] and fish. We had to spend our money within our means and in local markets that had affordable commodities. I was on a journey that was full of challenges that called for tested perseverance. When I reflect back on it, it reminds me of what Mollica describes as one of his father's favorite expressions, "Don't worry. It's going to get worse" (Mollica, 2006).

When people leave their countries for safety, usually, they leave unexpectedly because the calamities that come to them are unexpected. When faced with such calamities, they simply flee for their lives in disarray. They can only take what they find in their immediate surroundings. Sometimes people leave without knowing where they have left their valuables, even their children. In my own case, I left with only one son; I left everything else behind. As is common with many young wives, my experience of being a young wife married at 23, to the youngest

MP in the country who was elected at 26 years and four years later was ousted; we had not learned much in the short time of only four and a half years in leadership.

My only experience with how people live in poverty had been gained through my involvement with the rural community women's lives. This experience ended up preparing me for the unknown, working with people who had suffered war, displacement and traumas during the Rwenzururu's 20 years of bitterness. Now here I was, living in a new environment that was harsh and unwelcoming, and I had to learn new ways of living despite my inhospitable surroundings.

In search of a new home in Congo

Immigration from one country to another in search of safety or economic prosperity is not a new phenomenon. In my case after my husband had left Uganda to Congo, I could not cope under the hardships and horrible conditions of poverty, sicknesses and loneliness without the support of my husband who was not in the country. I chose to follow him in the Democratic Republic of Congo (DRC). Following him was a venture of determination to go and face the unknown world. I was going to face a challenge of learning new things, like a new baby learning to walk.

The conditions of living poor

Searching for new life in a new country is always full of uncertainty. There are feelings of self-pity or condemnation about the past, especially if the future is not promising. In search of a new home, I had to create new horizons in order to survive with my family. Accommodation was difficult to find in this new world, especially where financial constraints were also an issue for us to afford even a one bedroom apartment. In the Democratic Republic of Congo-then Zaire, life was not all that easy, especially because of the political instabilities at the time. The civilians were not happy with their long serving dictator Martial Mobutu Sese Seko Kuku Ngwendo Wa Zabanga.

There were demonstrations all over the country with a lot of looting and killings on the streets. As mentioned before, I left everything behind in Uganda. In order to survive in this new ordeal of searching for a new home, I had to accept the reality of life, as an ordinary woman who had to fit in. My plan to succeed in this environment was to interact with some of the local women in this community; some of whom were affluent with husbands having good jobs. These women would invite me to go with them for shopping, but where would I get the finances to go shopping?

There were times when these women spoke in French, the official language of the DRC, and this really put me off. I felt lost and a sense of insecurity around them. I kept asking myself, do I have any future, or did it end with my past life? Each day that went by I questioned whether there was any hope for me to ever get out of this situation because I had nothing to keep me busy. Each day that came by, I sat at home only to feed my mind with regrets of why I ever chose to leave my country. To make matters worse, we were financially in a crisis. We depended on the little money that we had saved from some of the property that we sold when we were still in Uganda.

When the women who had asked me to go with them to the market/shopping came back, they displayed what they bought, and the different types of food they would prepare for their families. What would I display for my husband and child? I wish I could tell you these weren't true stories. The women I describe here were my neighbors I thought were going to be my friends. Who is your neighbor or friend in this case? I assume the one who shares your pain and joy is that person whom you will call friend. A friend is someone who treats you well in terms of how you also treat them. The women that came to me had homes; they had families, relatives and places they called their own. What was mine in this whole picture? I was virtually in exile, an exiled woman whose hope was shattered by the politics of my home country, Uganda.

The truth is that my life as a refugee woman who was used to being driven around, participated in social and developmental issues was brought to a test. More disappointing was seeing my husband who was a member of parliament, represented his people in the highest assembly of government, completely powerless. There was nothing that would keep my husband busy while I went to the markets to sell charcoal for financial survival. Charles Stanley in his monthly magazine "In Touch, Aug.2007" points out that:

Although we physically function in the present, we aren't restricted to the now when it comes to our thoughts. We can

41

live in the future, always thinking about what's coming next, or in the present, constantly processing today's events. And some regularly live in the past, which can create problems. It is easy to get stuck in days gone by, dwelling on old hurts and feelings of guilt. True, it can sometimes seem almost impossible to let go of past mistakes and errors in judgment. When that is the case, pangs of remorse wrap around our minds like chains, preventing us from moving forward and anchoring us to feelings of condemnation (p.36).

I constantly questioned why I became the victim of political instability when I had so much ahead of me that I needed to accomplish. My husband had joined politics before we got married. Oh, he should have known how I blamed him for every pain I endured! We were still fiancées at the time when he joined politics. What I failed to remember was that during the good days, I did not blame him for being a politician or for the respect and honor people gave me by virtue of being a wife of a member of parliament. Now that I was in this situation, he became the culprit. However, never at any point did I ever show him such frustrations. I handled my emotions without being overtly expressive, but calmly talked about our frustrations while supporting each other.

It is true that in every situation that we face, there will always be the scapegoat. It is well known that in the Garden of Eden, when Adam and Eve were asked by God why they were hiding after they had eaten the forbidden fruit, both of them had reason to pass blame on to someone else. Adam put the blame on the woman God had given him in the Garden. He said, the "woman" God gave him, gave him the fruit to eat. He blamed God that if you had not given me this woman, I would not have eaten the forbidden fruit. Eve on the contrary was ready to defend herself regarding the "snake that tricked her to eat the fruit" (Genesis NIV).

Yes, we all bear witness to blaming others for our own mistakes, pains or wrongful acts. Blaming has no ending point to it! I questioned why I became the victim of politics when innocent. I am that person who knows how to hide my emotions; and more specifically, I did not want my husband to bear the burden of feeling my emotional pains of this internal trauma of our situation.

Herman explains: Relieving a trauma may offer an opportunity for mastery, but most survivors do not consciously seek or welcome the opportunity. Rather, they dread and fear it. Reliving a traumatic experience, whether in the form of intrusive memories, dreams, or actions, carries with it the emotional intensity of the original event" (1997: 42). I did not want to dread my social disconnection, but tried to reach out for some connections in order to build a social network. I did this by simply creating a mechanism of going to the local church and gave a smile to whichever woman looked approachable. Indeed, this plan worked, I got some connections through this approach.

The connection with local people

In this new environment, it was important that I build some connections with the local people. However, building an identity in this new environment was very challenging, especially where mastering local languages was a hurdle of its own. In this new environment, both my husband and I had to accept the reality that we were no longer political figures and had to live like everybody else in this new country. Despite a small cluster of local women that I had built alliances with, one particular woman with whom we spoke the same language, developed a strong interest in me. She became my mentor in this new environment. She guided me and showed me places I could go to buy food. She did not only become a mentor, but a dear friend who went above and beyond her boundaries. She helped me in every aspect of life as I needed. Indeed, she was a true friend. I could not go places without her because of language problems. She did the talking, price bargaining when we went to buy food. Later, she advised me to start crossing over into the nearby country of Rwanda to bring goods back into Congo for sale.

At the time of our stay in Congo, the government was going through a lot of opposition and there were riots and demonstrations all over the country. There were shootings on the streets and life became so tense for us. We had to get used to another reminder of what we had just escaped from in our country Uganda. Despite the unrest, my friend continued to encourage me to do vending across the border with Rwanda. I did not speak Kinyarwanda nor did I speak French, if I chose to do business across borders, I had to learn both languages.

My friend did not speak either language. She spoke the local language, Kiswahili and her mother tongue, Kinandi, which we used to communicate with each other. Although we did not have enough capital to start a business, my friend and I took the first adventure and crossed over into Rwanda, which was about five kilometers from Goma, the city in Congo where we lived. On a given market day when many vendors crossed over into Rwanda for business, we also had to go on foot. Not being a businessperson and with no trading experience, I had to learn to live a new life style just to fit in. In this new endeavor, I realized having someone who encourages you can take one beyond the horizons ever experienced. It was through someone who held my hand and guided me that I managed to take another adventure in life, doing business that would alleviate our financial situation.

The business that resurrected past traumatic memories

One Tuesday morning in August, 1988, I prepared myself for a new adventure; starting a business that I felt would get us out of poverty. Prior to that morning, my friend prepared me, demonstrated to me how Congolese business women dress, and where to stash money when crossing over into Rwanda. It was a cloudy, foggy and cold morning; we prepared ourselves to cross over into Rwanda. One could barely see someone one meter away, much less the border security dressed in uniform. Traffic was a mix of market vendors, and heavy trucks carrying goods to and from Rwanda. The commotion around the border was intimidating for me personally. I felt uneasy seeing images of civilians and Rwandese custom guards dressed in army uniform. The obvious intimidation was the way the guards searched women's undergarments looking for money. These images made me want to discontinue my journey. Where was women's privacy in this whole situation?

To my amazement, many of the women that were searched appeared not bothered. It was like something they were familiar with. I did not want to go through this. I felt sick to my stomach. As soon as we lined up on the boarder of Congo and Rwanda to be checked, I felt sick to the point that it was very difficult for me to walk. My friend was surprised to see me in this state. Someone who came while normal, and now within five minutes in this new environment I was totally in a different state of mind! I was reliving my past experience when the Uganda government was overthrown, and the time when the Bishop was slapped by the mob while taking me to my parents.

The reality is, when traumatic experiences always impact people negatively. Even the slightest cue of the situation will cause a lot of panic. The experience revoked traumatic memories. My friend asked me what had happened, but I could not speak. I could not understand either what had happened. The Rwandese border guards continued with their operation searching everyone that was going to the market. When they came to me, it was the same pattern of searching as they did to other women; the experience of searching my bra made me very uncomfortable because, I was not familiar with this kind of practice.

Not knowing how to stash away money, the customs officers took most of my money I had. I am not sure if they had recognized that I was not familiar with business techniques. People in both countries walked boldly and I believe the soldiers had seen the terrified face of this refugee woman, who they assumed would not be able to negotiate her free and safe passage into Rwanda with them as other women did. Language was a factor which complicated matters. I was not able to defend myself by not allowing them to take all my money. We finally crossed into Rwanda and could hardly walk or talk.

My friend was horrified by the mysterious sickness that had just hit me so instantly. I was left with very little money. Since unlike me, my friend still had her money, she did the shopping while I laid down. I was feeling very dizzy and sick most of the time while in the market.

At that time none of us could understand what was wrong with me. After three hours in the market, it was again time to go back to Goma, Congo. With the money that we had left, we bought two full loaded bags of clothes. Throughout the whole time we were in the market, my mind was racing about how I was again going to face those soldiers at the border. I was like a walking zombie not knowing about the mysterious sickness that had hit me. Even standing up to try and walk was difficult. I felt like I was carrying a load on my head, which I have come to understand as symptoms of stress.

I had been previously traumatized and feared seeing anybody with a machete, military uniform or anything associated with what I had witnessed the night of July 26, 1986. I was traumatized and left with effects of fear, depression and anger. With these experiences still fresh in my mind, I feared the worst when I came face to face with the soldiers at the Border of Rwanda and Congo. Herman (1997) explains the effects of re-traumatization as follows:

> People subjected to prolonged, repeated trauma develop an insidious, progressive form of post-traumatic stress disorder that invades and erodes the personality. While the victim of a single

acute trauma may feel after the event that she is not herself, the victim of chronic trauma may feel herself to be changed irrevocably, or she may lose the sense that she has any self at all. The worst fear of any traumatized person is that the moment of horror will recur-and this fear is realized in victims of chronic abuse (p. 86).

And indeed, this was my situation. My situation on the border was a reminder that I was again at war with my past reality during the overthrow of the Ugandan government, when the mob invaded my house. Was I ready to relive my past after I thought I had escaped those memories by fleeing the country? Not really. It was very unfortunate that I continuously felt sick. Each time I saw a uniformed man, I shrunk to my nerves as though I had seen an enemy that I dreaded. How I desired that the fear and nervousness could disappear, but nothing happened. It was the beginning of a long journey of traumatic memories of fear and anxiety.

I developed panic attacks. Each time something banged on the wall or something fell off to the ground, or even children crying or shouting, I went into a deep anxiety attack and fear. I was now faced with a sickness that I did not understand. I developed constant headaches where my husband could do nothing to help me in this foreign country. He also became helpless, especially seeing that I had developed a mysterious sickness that had no identification or diagnosis.

I had no idea about Post-Traumatic Stress Disorder until I did my Masters of Social Work. It was only then, years later that I was able to understand what I had experienced after the border incident. Herman, J. (1997) further explains that:

Reliving a trauma may offer an opportunity for mastery, but most survivors do not consciously seek or welcome the opportunity. Rather, they dread and fear it. Reliving a traumatic experience, whether in the form of intrusive memories, dreams, or actions, carries with it the emotional intensity of the original event. The survivor is continually buffeted by terror and rage... Because reliving a traumatic experience provokes such intense emotional distress; traumatized people go to great lengths to avoid it. The effort to word off intrusive symptoms, though self-protective in intent, further aggravates the post-traumatic syndrome, for the attempt to avoid reliving the trauma too often results in a narrowing of consciousness, a withdrawal from engagement with others, and an impoverished life (p.42).

I decided to drop the idea of going anywhere around the city in fear that I might have similar experiences as that at Gisenyi-Rwanda border.

A friend who never gave up on me

Friendship stands challenging moments and will last even during the most difficult times. I got that friendship from a woman who never gave up on me, and has remained a friend to this day. My friend did not want to give up on me and remained hopeful that I continue with the Rwanda business of getting more clothes. It was very difficult to even take the first load to the markets to sell. Each time I attempted to go to these public arenas, I was not at peace. I feared to accidentally meet people who knew me and could inform Ugandan authorities where we were. Unfortunately my friend was not aware of this internal turmoil I was experiencing. She was only a good person who wanted to do what she felt was best for me. She did not want me to remain isolated and unengaged in social activities which would distract me from emotional and psychological stress. I did as she advised.

I recall one market day, I was selling the second hand clothes I bought from Rwanda. I saw someone I thought was from Uganda. I tried to disguise myself and covered my face with a sackcloth. Tears rolled down my cheeks feeling the shame of how a woman, who used to dream big, was brought to this level of a market vendor! I remained fearful of anybody that resembled my country people the rest of the business day. It did not take long before I quit this public association. This was not the kind of life I intended to live the rest of my stay in exile. Besides, I had also developed anger towards my husband.

I grew up knowing that it was the man's responsibility to look after the family and the wife was to be a housekeeper. Was I right or was it only frustrations that brought all these feelings? I felt the rational of having these feelings because, that is what I saw my father do! I felt there was no justice for me in this whole arrangement. My interpretation of the situation was that it was not my responsibility to be looking for food and vending for the three of us, but my husband's. In many cases, I came from the market with intentions of telling my husband to be responsible for cooking for the family while I did the business. This would be an insult to a man who was from a culture where men are usually not responsible for cooking. Moreover, we were not living a luxurious life style in houses with electricity, where I would ask him to put on the stove and cook. It was also going to be difficult under our circumstances to see my husband get down on his knees and begin making the fire on the wooden stove. It would be an embarrassment and insult for me to do this to my husband. This is not what was expected of men in my culture!

Even though I was in exile, I was a busy woman also making babies. I was pregnant with my third son. One might ask whether we knew about family planning. The answer is "yes" I knew. However, where could I have accessed family planning facilities when I was a refugee who knew nothing about the medical system of the new host country? Besides, there was nobody I trusted to show me places. Even if this was the case, I doubt I could have gone for family planning services. It is only in the Western World that these places can easily be accessible. Moreover, it was not easy to talk to someone with whom I had not developed a rapport to discuss birth control issues. My friend whom I had just developed friendship did not believe in birth control. Furthermore, it was a different culture than where I came from.

My friend did not want to give up the idea of doing business and insisted that we go one more time. This time, the border guard talked to me in French, which I could not understand. They as well spoke in another local language I did not understand either. I was confused and could not understand whether they were talking about me or what else they were talking about. My friend explained to the uniformed man, that I was a Ugandan living in Goma, Congo. Wow, it sounded as though my friend was just putting fire on my head, for my identity had just been exposed! I felt heaviness in my chest and on my head as though I was carrying a stone.

I pretended as if nothing had happened, but all in vain. What was running through my mind was, why could my friend betray me to the point of disclosing my nationality? My friend had no idea these were questions racing in my mind. I feared for the worst; to be deported to Uganda. I wondered why my friend did this to me. Did she know what she was putting me through? My friend was very spiritual. She trusted nothing would happen to me because we trusted in God who is always by our side. When you are in fear for your life, sometimes in those instances, it becomes harder to trust there is a supernatural power that will protect you. My legs became feeble as we were being checked. Again, more money was taken from me, this time it was a bribe/token as they call it in some of these countries.

I gave what I had. The unfortunate part is that I didn't know the local currency value. Whatever amount I had was what I gave. When we finally counted how much I was left with, my friend was shocked when I told her that I had given everything. It was a shock to her because I had not learnt from my first encounter with the border control officers. I explained to my friend my fear when she told the soldier that I was a Ugandan. She rebuked me and reminded me how she had repeatedly told me to not entertain fear. Easier said than done! I looked at her with anger and pity at the same time because, I knew this woman did not know the psychological torment I was going through.

The constant fear left me with two choices, to drop the idea of doing business across the border or to look for an alternative. I was nervous each time I had memories of crossing into Rwanda; I felt sick. First of all, I was not a businesswoman when we were still in Uganda, but a social person who was passionate about the lives of poor women. Here I was in this new situation where I faced challenges of not knowing what the next day would bring for me.

My husband could not imagine to begin going out to the market with me either. Oh, that would have been embarrassing enough for me to see my husband in such a situation. After two attempts of going across the border, I felt it was too risky for me to continue with this arrangement. The business that I had engaged in was not going well. It was not easy to reconstruct my life and identity in exile; looking at the circumstances that surrounded me. Crossing the border often meant that the life must be reconstructed in circumstances and cultures alien to my own.

Surely did I have to go through this discomfort? I would say, yes, who else did I want to go through this experience? What I did not understand then was that global and local conflicts often emerge due to sociopolitical changes. Many of these changes entail negative consequences for women, usually in the form of violence against them. The nature of political power in many developing countries such as Uganda is characterized by political exclusion through single party, and state dominated authoritarian rule. This is a key source of conflict. It is generally common in each case that political victory assumes a 'winner takes it all' approach with respect to wealth, resources, patronage, prestige and the prerogative of office.

In the case of the political situation that I was coming from, it was a multiparty system, which had fallowed Idi Amin's nine-year regime. People were very angry and dissatisfied with the system, thus resulting in a coup d'état of the government we worked for. There were those who rejoiced and others who fell victims of circumstances. In most cases, one finds that countries that have been hurt so much, there will always be political and economic power heavily centralized and monopolized; resulting in massive corruption, nepotism, tribalism and abuse of office. When all these are aggregated, there is always dissatisfaction resulting in political upheaval. However, the person that suffers the most is the innocent civilian, especially women and children. The healing had not yet happened in this part of the country such that anyone who was in the previous regime had to run for their lives. We had become the culprits.

In my case, there was insecurity and fear of not knowing whether both my husband and I would be deported to Uganda. This experience of being a refugee was very traumatizing. The breakdown of a family unit, familiar social connections and economic constraints that I experienced meant having even fewer support networks and possessions. We needed assurance from people that things would be okay, but that assurance was not there because of the limited social network! The Dalai Lama (2007 p.86) writes, "We know, for example, how comfort and reassurance can help dispel fear. Similarly, those forms of counseling can help alleviate depression."

There were many factors that contributed to this depression. In fact, constructing the life experiences of immigrant and refugee families is a series of transitions, with each stage presenting a myriad of challenges and opportunities. For us as a family, there were no glimpses of opportunities. Each time and moment, my husband and I were consistently making new decisions that would forever change our lives. While each decision carried uncertainties, there were also moments where we remained hopeful that maybe at one time our lives would be better if we continued with what we were focusing on, relocating to a country that was safe!

Echoing the Dalai Lama (2007), we can conceive of the nature of mind in terms of the water in a lake. When the water is stirred up by a storm, the mud from the lake's bottom clouds it, making it appear opaque. But the nature of the water is not dirty. When the storm passes, the mud settles and the water is left clear once again (Ibid). What this quote explains to me is that we do not need to be controlled by our fears and emotions, but only to remain with a positive attitude. This is what my husband and I did.

In my professional experience, I have worked with many refugees, every one of them have their unique way they react to fear. The plight under which they fled for safety and the underlying reasons for persecution they escaped contribute to their unique reason for fear. In my case, it was dire poverty that triggered the emotions of fear as I tried every possible means to work on a business that did not look promising. Through this experience, I now look at life from a different perspective, with an attitude of gratitude for what I have been blessed with, especially since I came to live in Canada, a country that has privileges that I could not find in my exile life in Congo. There will be times of sorrow, disappointments and failures, which will make us realize the privileges we have or, even the growth such situations bring. I can now look back over my life and tell you that some of the best things I have enjoyed or that have come my way were also the very things that caused severe pain, heartache, and suffering. I have come to understand that what may seem to be a grave disappointment can also become a doorway to blessings. In most cases, we may not know until sometime later, the good that has come in our lives, through times of brokenness and despair. I will explain this later in the next chapter why some of our disappointments and brokenness have brought joy as I now work with families that have had their own experiences of life's trauma; and also as I work with other refugee women in my now home country, Canada.

Learning new survival strategies

Life continued to be that of adventures from border crossing to local vending. I started a different business of selling food products because I did not want to continue facing situations that reminded me of my past experiences. Doing business locally would allow me to deal with my fears of uniformed armed men. Starting a local business was not easy either. I was again faced with another challenge of a new adventure of selling food products. Well, such venture came with its own struggles that had more psychological torture. For instance, I experienced mental torture while on the look-out for who might be a Ugandan doing business locally since we stayed close to Uganda. People in Uganda usually bought their products from Goma in DRC. Secondly, there was the shame of seeing myself, a wife of a former member of parliament selling food products in the local market, not knowing who my customers might be. Consequently, I found that the market where I sold my products was bigger than I anticipated. I started competing with women vendors who had established businesses and with huge connections, which I did not have. As mentioned before, I sat in the market and got no customers. More disappointingly, was the fact that I was always cautious of people who might know who I was. There was constant covering of my face from people whom I felt were familiar, to avoid the spread rumors about what we were doing in Congo. In many instances, I went to the market without selling anything. We ended up eating everything without any profit. The following month would come and we would be expected to pay rent, with no money to do so. The panic was even worse than that of not selling my food products. I was already pregnant and expecting any time soon, and worrying was not healthy for the baby.

There was nowhere to go for social support in order for me to alleviate the stress. It is evident that social connections can open up new opportunities for survival, especially when faced with financial and emotional trauma. Writing this book, I can feel the horrible experience of being in exile where you find yourself totally disconnected from any familiar environment for support. It is strangely compelling to think about the horrible experiences that one goes through.

After realizing that we were at our wits end, we decided to relocate to another place, close to my home country, Uganda. The reasoning was that we would be near relatives that could help with food and free rent. Following my unsatisfactory journey journey of business adventures, I decided to do a different type of business. I felt that the only means I could earn a living in this new home was to conduct myself like Congolese women. Most of the women in this country are very enterprising! I spoke to the mother of the host family where we had relocated about the issue of buying charcoal, which is commonly used in every household as a means of local firewood for cooking. It is important to note that I come from a previously British colonial country and usually, with the British system, we are not as aggressive as French speaking/Belgium colonized countries. I tried to fit between the two different imperially influenced cultures, negotiating my identity as a Ugandan/former British subject and now Congolese/Belgium subject. Like many refugee women who are trying to negotiate their identity have experienced, it wasn't easy for me.   These French-speaking women were a bit aggressive when it came to doing business. In order for me to do business like them in this new society, I needed to be aggressive as well. I really wanted to be proactively involved in some productive activities despite being very pregnant. One woman shares her situation of not wanting to be idle. Her narrative confirms what I experienced in this country.

African women don't like to sit at home and do nothing. We are used to work. We go to farms, we make our farms, we trade, we go in the markets, and then, those who are educated they go to work in the offices, teaching, all those things (Int.12, Wasik, 2006).

Being proactive helps these women keep from thinking about their problems. This is what drove me to do something that would distract me from the fear of the unknown. Dossa (2004) explains in her book, Politics and Poetics of Migration about one refugee's experience, "Life would be easier for me if I could find a job. I would like to be active in my life and have a job" (p.78). These were the same thoughts that I had while negotiating between my socioeconomic and my identity in Congo. I was desperate to get anything to lay my hands on to keep me busy and distract my emotional feelings and engage in something tangible, get some small business that would relieve me of the tension of being poor and not productive in my new society.

Reconstructing my life to suit the standards of this new home was equally testing as it was when I decided to leave my home country, Uganda. How could I change from a modest woman to a radical/ aggressive woman when I was still faced with the challenge of learning a new language? In this process, I was also bombarded with memories of how life used to be, a common phenomenon with anybody who is on the crosswalk of negotiating two identities.

Dossa (2005) continues to elaborate on experiences that many immigrant and refugee women encounter. She explains how it is a common theme of displacement where pain and suffering is like the soft knife of politics, which can bring particular trajectories in women's lives. It is true that women's most intense experiences of pain are felt in every country where they take refuge. No one ever wants to go through hardships as a result of these so-called soft knives of politics. One would rather find it easier to live in turmoil back in their countries of origin than to live a life where you do not have any choice.

Coming back to my charcoal business, the host mother had some connections in the Ituri forest of the Mbute people who were well known for charcoal trade. It was a trip that would take us two hours walk before we reached these forests where the Mbute people lived. The first time I tried this adventure, I was not fearful that I might find soldiers like the Rwanda/Gisenyi encounter. What was problematic and tedious was the journey to and from.

The first day I bought a sack of about 30 Kilograms of charcoal, carried it on my back, and walked about 30 Kilometers back to where I lived. I had not done this in years, carrying a heavy load on my back and walking such a long distance was unheard of. The first trip had such a huge toll on my health. I was sick with muscle pains, headache and fever. Gladly, people bought my charcoal and within three days, the sack of charcoal had all been sold out. I tried this adventure about four times, but each time I came back, I was so sick that all the profit I got was spent on medication because of fever. I recall one night after my journey back from the Ituri forest; I had high fever and feared I was going to die. I needed someone to comfort me or speak a word of encouragement that I would be okay. One night, I woke my five year old son, and told him to call the host mother for me. We were living in the same house, but because I was so sick, I had gone to bed earlier than everybody. My son went and called the host mother.

Unfortunately, it took this woman over thirty minutes before she came to attend to me. I felt neglected and not cared for. Emotions of not having my husband around brought a lot of mixed memories. All the while, my husband had gone to Kinshasa the capital city to negotiate our resettlement with the United Nations High Commission for Refugees (UNHCR). Kinsasha was like another world from where we lived because for me to communicate with him, it would take two months before I received mail from him.

The emotional feelings of being neglected almost pushed me into panic mode. I depended on this woman and could not understand why she simply ignored me when she knew that I have been sick for over a week. She could not take time to find out what the problem was. I got out of the house and went to a nearby nurse, who had a private clinic in her house. She nursed me after she had found that my body temperature was too high. She treated me for malaria without taking any blood sample. I had feared to go to this woman because of her professional malpractice.

She customarily used the same needle to inject more than one patient. This incident happened at the time that HIV/AIDS epidemic had spread in many parts of the country. You should have seen the fear on my face. It was like a sheep that was taking itself to the slaughter house. As a matter of fact, I had not heard any reports of people getting the virus as a result of her practice. I was only fearful that this might be an easy way for me to contract the virus. I was vulnerable and I had no other clinic in the neighborhood that I could go to at night.

This was a clinic where I had taken my two sons for treatment before, but only trusted that there was nothing that had happened to them. After the treatment, I went back to the house, which was just next-door. As I arrived in the house, the host mother had known that I had gone to the neighbor's clinic for treatment. While at the clinic, I kept thinking that maybe someone would come to check on me, but there was nobody. I was frustrated and left with the feeling of isolation as I had experienced before. There were mixed feelings of anger and regrets how people I had trusted could ignore me to this extent. My experience has been that when you know that there are people who care when you are in need, the burden is usually lighter than when you are left entirely on your own.

Support and care have been part of my practice during my experiences working with people who have had traumatic experiences. The feeling of knowing that there are people who care and say encouraging words is healing for people who go through traumatic experiences. I have learnt this in my practice, working with people who have had all sorts of traumatic experiences, from loss of beloved ones, brain injury or displacement. Any simple word of support that I say to my clients, I sense a change of attitude in their behavior and a smile that rejuvenates from depression, anger, frustration and withdrawal to a feeling of joy and happiness. A listening ear is enough antidote to anyone who has experienced some sort of emotional, psychological and physical trauma. Many do not need medication, but only the empathy/sympathy that they get from people who understand their situations.

In my work with people from different walks of life, especially women that have had traumatic experiences, I have learnt to respond quickly when someone calls for help. You might find that when you delay to respond to a call, someone might have already gotten into major trouble or a serious situation that could otherwise have been avoided. What amazes me is how that experience has shaped my current profession in working with the vulnerable and traumatized populations.

Some of the women I have worked with for a long time, and have developed a good rapport with me, respond with insults and angry outbursts when something goes wrong for them or I don't fully pay attention as they would have wanted. I have learnt not to take such experiences personally, but as a means of wanting someone that they have trusted to really give undivided attention that will give these hurting women some hope and motivation to face the next day with a clear and positive attitude. The experience with my host mother was painful, but it has also become a reminder for me whenever I am called to attend to my patients.

I know that there are many women out there suffering in silence or acting out their pain in very serious and destructive ways. What will happen to these women, I wonder? I know that not all of us are as vulnerable or strong as society assumes. In our own way, we each have floundering emotional needs to have someone to acknowledge our feelings, brokenness and to desperately try to understand our pains or the loss of our identity has meant. I know some of us have discovered new possibilities within ourselves and in our lives. We feel empowered as a result of our strength and positive attitude that we forged. However, in writing my personal journey, it has become clear that vulnerable and traumatized women and children and many countless other victims of disruption/ displacement need more, "a listening ear."

Fear after Treatment

After my treatment with this nurse, I wrestled with the hygienic issues in this woman's clinic. In previous visits to her house, I had seen her use the same needle for about five children who were sick with malaria, including my own two sons. The fear almost killed me. The outside appearance did not depict the internal turmoil that I was wrestling with regarding the treatments that my family received from this community nurse. There were fears of contracting HIV/AIDS about which I did not have much education, except its symptoms such as rashes on the skin, dry cough, diarrhea, and weight loss. Each time I saw a rash or a small pimple on my skin or my sons' skin, I would fall into a panic. If I lost some pounds or my children lost weight, I would have sleepless nights that we had got the virus. About thirty years ago, in my country anybody who had these identified symptoms, was labeled to have had (*slim*), meaning HIV/AIDS positive. Did I want to go through this in this new country? I kept myself observant over such symptoms on all the three of us.

Unfortunately, my children continued to fall sick with malaria under the circumstances of lack of medical facilities in the community. Each day that passed by, there were deaths of little children due to malaria. The fear intensified although I had to hold on to my faith that God would see me through. I recall one neighbor who always passed by and found me crying in the room while praying that God's miracle would happen for me to get out of this situation. What I needed to hear were words of encouragement that would take me through the next month or even a year.

Those words of encouragement again came from my friend who supported and guided me with the Gisenyi, Rwanda business. She had moved to this part of the country just as we had relocated from Goma. She was indeed my friend who shared my pain! Too this day, we have continued to be friends and have met so many times and rejoiced over her perseverance to support me when I was in exile. Thankfully, I was able to rejoice that our family was still intact despite children on the block dying very often. This gave me courage to look at things from a positive perspective. In this situation where I felt as though I was trapped, I had to choose to stay enthusiastic and positive about life, and stand up on the inside no matter what the outside looked like.

Remaining with this attitude meant that I had to stay enthusiastic, passionate, excited about the next day, even when there was nothing to be excited about; and then full of hope that life would be better, no matter the odds that I was faced with. It also meant that I had to make up my mind that I was not going to give up or quit on what I knew lay ahead of me, joining my husband in the capital city. This positive attitude became my driving force, to not allow my outside circumstances change me while I stay down on the inside, about everything that was going on in my life. Realistically, before I could get up on the outside, I had to get up on the inside (Meyer, 2008).

I had to say no to that which would pollute my mind with worries, and I had to quit condemning myself that I was the cause of all the problems about me. In most cases, victims of circumstances always blame themselves for situations beyond their control. There was no need for condemning myself for what surrounded me, which was displeasing in many instances. To remain with this attitude was a choice that I had to make. It was my choice to either remain engraved in my pain or cry where the cry would not take me anywhere. Osteen (2005) writes:

> When you get up in the morning, you can choose to be happy
> and enjoy that day, or you can choose to be unhappy and go

around with a sour attitude. It's up to you. If you make the mistake of allowing your circumstances to dictate your happiness, then you risk [developing health problems such as depression, anxiety and panic attacks] (pp. 25).

In this case, I felt that the only way to live a happy life was to accept what my fellow church women I had connected with offered me without any remorsefulness or resentment towards them. Resent them by the way they dressed, their mannerism, or how they talked about their extended families, of which I did not have. The fact that they accepted me as a fellow believer was good enough to be thankful to them because, I had a cluster of women who would smile with me when I needed to!

Dress became an issue. In Congo, women dress up in their local traditional attires, which were usually ranked according to status. Those whose husbands were well to do, have a different class of attire called "super wax" or "Hollandaise." If a woman is seen dressed in any of these categories, you were easily identified with which class category you come from. The host mother gave me clothes as she saw the need, to ensure that I did not look out of place. Unfortunately they could not fit me because I had lost weight. However, in order for me to blend in this culture, I was obliged to dress like the local women. Moreover, dressing like them, did not relieve me of my internal conflict of identity that I was struggling with as a "Ugandan refugee woman" on the block. Identity shapes the way you live and also brings meaning to everything that you do.

This life did not appear to bring any glimpse of hope about what I had dreamt to be. How could I revive my ambitions of getting out of this situation looking at the challenge that lay ahead, financial constraints, and a support network? Jaynes (2004) points out:

One thing I love about children is that you never have to remind them to dream. There is always more to discover, worlds to be explored, and conquests to be made. We never made to remind a child to want more. The doors of their hearts fling open to welcome all that life has to offer. Children can keep dreaming and dreaming without giving up on their dreams. If they want to build a toy car one evening, they will wake up the next morning wanting to work on the same dream until they finally achieve what they had started (p.226).

I wished I had the same courage and determination as that of kids. I felt my dreams completely erased and shattered by these erroneous situations. Some people have had shattered dreams and others have had restored dreams; I have had both. When my dreams were shattered, I depended on prayers. I grew deeper in my spiritual belief. I could not do anything, but to trust that there is a God who answers prayers. I fasted and prayed, waiting to get a break through. Indeed life was tested with the lowest times. The only thing I clung on was my faith.

In my struggle with my new identity, I felt the conditions in the refugee camp would have been better than being a burden to the family that was looking after us. However, I think this was an illusion as one woman points out:

To be in a refugee camp is not easy. In the refugee camp, there is a problem of fighting for food, no morale because you are not sure of what you will eat for the next day. African camps are not the best camps to live in. There are all sorts of sickness that can kill you any minute. In the refugee camp, they only supplied food twice a week and that was not really food!! It was maize meal. For example in the refugee camp in Kenya Kakuma camp, it is just a problem and it is one of the largest camps in the world. There are so many insects that could kill you within a minute such as scorpions. Insects could bite us to the extent that many of the people fainted to die. You see white foam coming from your mouth. So many women lost their children. You enter the camp with 5 kids but when you leave, you leave with only 3 kids and the rest of the 2 are already dead in the camp (Pascaline focus group #. 3, 2008).

Another one comments:

…just to go in the refugee in the other country, Congo and when we were there, there was so many troubles because the people there got cholera because so many people sleep around, outside in the church, outside in the house. Whenever they just go and sleep there, they don't have food, they don't have any drink and they get disease and cholera killed so many people. People died around and we saw them and there were so many troubles at the time

because to get water and to get food was so hard (focus group #
1, 2007).

As recounted above in these narratives, some of the women that
experienced refugee life in Kakuma camp had their own stories of pain.
I was also facing it in the same way, but in a different manner, identity
crisis. The downside to my problem was that after such a constant
torment of the unknown, I developed panic attacks. I was always fearful
to be in the room by myself, or see a plane fly over in the sky above
my head. The fear became an added sickness to the constant malaria
fever that my family suffered from. It is unfortunate that I was not
knowledgeable about Post-traumatic Stress Disorder (PTSD), as I am
now. I was dizzy most of the time and did not have any appetite to eat.
Each morning I woke up, I felt like I was carrying a rock on my head.

The most traumatizing incident was the feeling of the fear of
airplanes. I lived in fear of the unknown. As Joan James (1986) points
out:

> Fear is learned through experience and training. Many of the
> experiences of life are tragic and traumatic, and they leave
> indelible impressions on the sensitive subconscious mind. This
> fear may surface at any time-even years later in what may seem
> unrelated circumstances, and is often mixed with anger and
> hatred (p.90).

This is exactly what happened to me after my Rwanda experience.

I finally stopped the whole idea of selling charcoal because I had a
place to live. The only problem I was faced with was the medical aspect
of my children feeling sick very often. Many times I found myself crying
and had to lock myself in my room, where I never wanted my children
to see me cry. This was life in exile in Congo! Dossa's book, *Politics and
Poetics of Immigration* (2004), explains that

> ...bodies are communicative by nature and hence they use stories
> to convey critical messages to the world. Stories make it possible
> for sufferers to position themselves as witnesses to their traumas,
> inviting audiences to reciprocate by becoming witnesses in turn.
> This is what gives the story power (p.129).

Indeed, some of the difficult situations that we go through can make us speak to many incidents that go untold, but the power that such messages carry when they are told may help the reader to understand the real life of those who are voiceless to express their experiences. Talking about my experience, I believe will be a healing power to even those who have never been uprooted from their own comfort zones, but dealing with their own emotional traumas that might be related to my experiences in a different way.

Depending on whether you left your home country by boat, by air, by road, or by water, the fact remains that it is a difficult adventure for immigrant and refugee women when they leave their home country unexpected to start a new life with lots of uncertainty. Mine was full of challenges of relocating from one place to another, while my family relationship with my husband was being run remotely. We hardly lived together for one year while in exile. Each time we tried to live together, we found ourselves separated by virtue of the circumstances that we faced like economic hardships and insecurity!

It was indeed hard to survive those situations while my husband lived in the capital city trying to negotiate means for us to get out of the country to a safe place. We both navigated life's circumstances trying to get our way out of the hardships in the DRC with endurance. Most of all, communication was not easy to be able to share with each other our pains and challenges in our own different ways. We both struggled to achieve one common goal, to get to a safer and greener place to live.

Connecting with my husband

One ordinary morning, I saw a man holding an envelope come to the place where I lived in exile, Beni DRC. I had been waiting for good news to come from my husband who had been living in the capital city for the previous two years. Everyone in the neighborhood watched this man as he asked one of the children that were playing on the roadside if they knew a person identified by my name. The child brought the man to the house, only to greet him with excitement after he had delivered the news that he was coming from the capital city and that he lived with my husband. He informed me that any time I will get news about my travel to join my husband. He left me some financial help that would keep me for some time.

After about two years of waiting up country to finally rejoin with my husband, I got the news that I had been waiting for, to reunite with my husband! It was April 1991, when I received a telegram from a small air field office, stating that they had four tickets for my family to travel to Kinshasa to join my husband. After all that I had experienced up-country, the dream came to pass! The Airline Company sent someone to deliver the tickets. To my amazement, there was a ticket for my oldest son, whom we had left in Uganda. We were to travel to Kinshasa on April 15, 1991, and the tickets arrived around the first week of the month. I was faced with a dilemma to bring this child from Uganda to Congo. Airline only operated on specific days in this part of the country.

This was an opportunity that came with a test. It was not easy to connect with the child we had left in Uganda, and if there was, I was unable to raise money to send someone to bring him. If this plan fails, this would be the end of us to ever connect as a family. Again, I turned to my faith. I prayed to my God for this opportunity to not come in vein and prayed that this should be the end of my torment. I cried that God would make a miracle for this poor family to get through this circumstance. It was not healthy for a family to be separated for such a long time with one child in Uganda, a mother with two children upcountry in Congo and a husband in the capital Kinshasa almost 1660 miles away.

While I was feeling desperate, a family friend came to visit us from Nairobi, Kenya. When he arrived he was surprised about the tickets. What also surprised him was that he did not know about the tickets; neither did my husband who was in Kinshasa. I explained to him how the child in Uganda was to be picked because he was included as part of this trip. Our friend was a refuge as we were. He did not have the money to help me send someone to Uganda to get the child. I was faced with the dilemma of getting this child to join us immediately or else we miss the plane to travel to Kinshasa. We kept in constant touch with the Airline Company to request them to at least wait for another week because we were faced with the challenge of this child in Uganda to arrive.

It is very inconceivable that I share this story about how a passenger could make an airline company cancel its commitments, just to wait for my son who was in Uganda! This is a true story and it happened, not because we asked, but by God's divine intervention that indeed the plane could not proceed with the scheduled arrangement. It had mechanical problems that delayed the process while I was also busy connecting with the family in Uganda for my son to join us.

While waiting for the child to join us, we were told that the plane got stuck in Bunia and that it might take another week before we could travel. This was a miracle as I had prayed. I saw my son, my father and brother, who had brought this little boy; we all shed tears of joy and excitement. My son was now seven and had grown shy for all the three years he had been without his parents. The first thing he said to me was "Mummy, I thought you had died." At this point, he did not even speak my mother tongue, but had learnt the local language of the place where he lived. Talk about the pain in the eyes of a mother! Many refugee women are faced with statements like this when they reunite with their children. As a mother, I was ecstatic to see my son.

I had had many moments of torment, and guilt, not knowing how he was doing, and what was going on in his life. After only two days of being with my father and brother they left to go back to Uganda. It was too painful to see them leave. I did not know when I would see them again. However, my father was happy that we were going to be a family unit as we were finally going to join my husband.

On May 1, 1991 two weeks after the scheduled travel time, the Airline finally was ready to embark on its scheduled flight after all my family was together. This story amazed everyone in my family to see how things fell in place as we had prayed. Although it may sound negative in many people's ears, but I had prayed for some mechanical problems to delay the flight. Indeed, each time we called to check with the company to give them an update about our situation, they would also assure us that the plane is still having some problems that needed to be fixed before it is put to service. I believe this was not by coincidence, but an act of a high power. My faith grew even stronger as I saw us board the plane to go and rejoin my husband.

The excitement on our faces could only be told by another person. Words cannot express how we saw the amazing grace of the high power. The four of us finally flew to Kinshasa with a sleep over in Goma. Goma is where we had our first connections with the Ugandan landlady who rented us a suite during our first year in Congo. When the women I used to hang out with saw me, the whole community had already been informed that I was traveling to the United States of America, although it was actually Canada where we were going. I had become skinnier than before I moved from this part of the country.

To the community women who came to see me at the place where we had the night, it meant that I was not eating well and not looked after. Outward beauty is highly respected in many parts of the African culture (Masinda and Kambere, 2008). If I were in Canada, this would be a good complement. However, in Africa it was a different matter. To be skinny is a sign of poverty or mistreatment from your husband. Such complaints were an added fear for either sickness as you may recall the nurse's clinic incident.

When a person is moving to a western country, it is a common tendency in many developing countries to treat that person with dignity because, there are illusions that money is *"collected on the streets"* meaning, getting rich instantly. Some of the women came to make their own requests according to their needs such as: as soon as you arrive, please send me money for a fridge, stove and some household essentials. I was so shocked because all this was news to me. Where did they get this information that people coming to live abroad collect money on the streets? My husband had extensively traveled abroad and had never told me that money was found on the streets as these neighbors narrated the situation to me. To this day, such illusions are still in many people's minds. In my interaction with some of the immigrant and refugee families, they have told me similar stories that were told to them and came to Canada with such anticipations. To their disappointments, things were not as they had been informed.

Despite my excitement to finally move out of a rural area, inwardly I was tormented by fear of flying. It was like hiding a secret, of being in prison and yet not wanting people to know that you are there. There were times when I longed to live in full freedom without this secret of flight fear. Living in fear is really dreadful. You can never be free of these internal feelings that even people close to you may never understand. As Dr. Stanley (2008) demonstrates, "Fear...can keep us boxed in and unwilling to venture into unknown territory [of liberty]". There are publications that describe what people who have had prior trauma experience. With such people any similar or sudden danger will sometimes overcome them with feelings of fear, helplessness, or horror. This is what I experienced for over seven years, instead of rejoicing in the victory of finally going to join my husband.

Finally, it was early in the morning of May 2, 1991 when we finally left for the airport to join my husband in the capital city- Kinshasa. I did not know where I was going nor did I have the address of where my husband lived in the city. My husband would not be at the airport since the plane had delayed more than two weeks from the time he knew. My friend who was to meet us at the airport had not arrived to meet us and I had totally depended on him for directions. There was no way I could get in touch with our friend due to poor communication. I depended on God's mercy throughout these travel arrangements. At the time Kinshasa had a population of about six million and it was going to be difficult to locate my husband. The only connection I had was an acquaintance of ours who had visited me from Kinshasa two years prior. I knew his name, but did not know where he lived in the city.

As we finally departed from Goma airport, I simply depended on the mercy of some business men who were also traveling to the capital city, Kinshasa. They spoke the local language that I knew. I told them my story of how I was going to join my husband, but with no directions to where he lived. I told them of someone called Mr. Muhindo Binabira, [*now deceased*] who worked with Mobil gas company and that this is the man that might direct me to my husband.

These men were happy to meet me with my three children. This encounter worked well for both parties. The men had more luggage and were only allowed to carry two suit cases. My children helped carrying some luggage for them. Some of the men spoke a little English and they were excited practicing it. I told them that my husband and I were going to live abroad, and most likely the United States as the women had stated. The mention of living abroad gave me some status and respect. Moreover, the fact that I spoke English was an added merit because, I was in a French speaking country. I told them how my husband was a Member of Parliament in the previous Ugandan regime. I hope this was not being proud. I had to do this because I was desperately in need of help for directions and speaking up about my previous status was meant to boost my standing.

To my amazement, as we were about to board the plane coming out of the lounge room, I saw our friend who was as nervous as we were coming through the crowds to meet us. We finally got the actual address and telephone number in case we got lost. The flight from Goma to Kinshasa took us five hours and the businessmen hired a taxi for us to take me to Mr. Binabire's house. We arrived at the house late at night when they were almost going to bed. He was shocked to see me with three kids. He took our stuff and put it in his car then drove us to where my husband lived. When we arrived at this friend's house, my two sons were thrilled to see this man and asked me if this was their father? I told them "No." Mr. Binabire asked me if I had been sick. My answer was "yes a little bit." He again commented, "You have lost weight more than the last two years I met you." This comment put me off. Losing weight in this part of the world is associated with poverty, sickness or malnutrition.

As mentioned earlier, in Africa, you don't want to be told that you look small or you have lost weight. It got to my nerves and started getting me worried again about the needle issue. We finally arrived at the residence where my husband lived. It was at night and we were not aware he had been waiting for three weeks. When he came to get our stuff from the car, he was shocked to be greeted by our son, Dan, whom we had left in Uganda. It was four years since he had last seen his son.

The excitement that was on Dan's face for meeting his father together with his family made both my husband and I shed tears of joy. The two boys clung to their father while my second son, who was a bit reserved watched and kept on saying, "Dad, dad, where were you all these years?" In the year 1991 - after each of us struggled with life; we finally reunited as a family. It was a moment that we knew as a family how the power of God really brought us together after all the ordeals that we had faced in our own different ways.

This ordeal of living upcountry in isolation from my husband was a testing time for me personally. The hardships of children getting sick every often, and most of all, the miracle of uniting with my son whom we had been separated from for over four years was as exciting as the time we finally united with my husband. The whole ordeal of getting our son from Uganda despite our financial circumstances was one act of the higher power that I could not take for granted. Joining my husband with our three boys in an environment that looked promising for our future life, was a moment that we all felt our dreams of a happy life was about to unfold. I was finally relieved to see my husband in good health and my children together again in a different environment smiling with joy and happiness.

My family in the Congo Capital City - Kinshasa

Many refugees have been traumatised by their experiences of torture – the torture of leaving their familiar surroundings and living in conditions that are unbearable. These experiences will have a profound impact on the family's sense of safety and identity, and settling in

Kinshasa placed a great deal of stress on our family due to improper accommodation. There was the struggle to settle into a new city, which was like another country that we had never lived in while trying to meet the basic survival needs.

When we arrived, we found my husband sharing a house with about 17 refugee men from mainly, Angola, Kenya and Uganda, who were under United Nations High Commission for Refugees (UNHCR) protection. I was the only woman among twenty men including my sons who lived in a five-bedroom house that was called "Mason De-passage" transition house. My husband was sharing a room with one boy, who had to give up his bed for our three boys to share. Three of our boys squeezed in one bed. We had to learn placing them in one bed without pushing each other to the ground, and survived these conditions for one year. This single room served as a bedroom, living room and as dining room. The children were very excited to be with their father and we were all happy to be a family unit again. It did not matter how we slept.

However, my only worry was the struggle with identity crisis. Living with nineteen men and being the only woman became problematic for me. Using one common kitchen and two bathrooms was challenging for me and caused some discomfort. The good side to this story is that these men in the Mason De-passage were respectful of us by virtue of being a family. They also loved my boys and looked after them as their very own. Keep in mind, in Africa it is the responsibility of everybody to look after each other's children. In the African culture, parenting is looked at as a community responsibility where everybody contributes in disciplining or feeding the child (Masinda & Kambere, 2008). In general, in Africa a child belongs to the community and "It takes a whole village to bring up a child." My children met boys whom they called brothers; they also met men whom they called uncles, according to the African culture.

After leaving in two different cultures, I have realized that this was a blessing for us to have people who were there to help us with parenting. In my current culture, this kind of parenting would be considered intrusive. Over 20 years that I have lived in the west, I have found people to be very individualistic and sometimes they get offended so easily if you dare to "interfere" with their family.

One morning while still in Kinshasa Congo, I did what most of us mothers usually do, when we try to assign responsibilities to our children, especially when we are busy with house chores. I asked our first son to do dishes as the first chore since he joined us. When he joined me, he was never expressive, but always cried quietly whenever he was hungry. He hadn't bonded much with me to freely express himself. The only way he communicated to me the two weeks after arriving from Uganda was to cry. Whatever this meant psychologically, I am yet to understand.

I had promised this boy that when we finally joined his father, life was going to be fine. What I was not knowledgeable about was the healing process that people need to undergo. Children, like adults also have their own way of healing after prolonged separation from their parents. My son had just joined me after over three years of not being together with his parents. He needed to go through the healing process. We needed to bond, and he needed unconditional love. Joyce Mayer (2008) says "Often, people do not allow themselves time to heal, or they heal improperly and become cynical. The emotional nourishment that comes from good relationships is cut off and the person starves in the soul" (p.22).

I believe this boy had just got the connection with his mother, but there was emotional healing that was still needed. It was like when a bone is broken; it must be realigned so as to heal well. Our son needed to first bond with both parents before we could begin treating him as though he had been with us the last four years. As it is customary in the African culture, a first born child is always expected to help out with house chores whenever possible for others to learn from them. This is exactly what I did after four weeks in Kinshasa. I asked this boy to do dishes. The boy never said anything, but did as instructed.

I was not knowledgeable about how emotionally children can be resentful especially when they begin to think of why they were left behind. I had forgotten about my own childhood separation and how I was affected. I was only concerned about my own joy of reuniting with my son. I was concerned about feeding my children, but neglected the psychological and emotional well-being of this young boy. There are very interesting publications that talk about the impact of emotional bonding.

I am not an expert to talk about this, neither is it the intention of my narrative. It is well documented that the capacity and desire to form emotional relationships is related to the organization and functioning of specific parts of the human brain. Just as the brain allows us to see, smell, taste, think, talk and move, it is the organ that allows us to love or not. Bonding is the process of forming an attachment. Just as bonding is the term used when gluing one object to another, bonding is using our emotional glue to become connected to another. In other words, bonding, therefore, involves a set of behaviors that will help lead to an emotional connection attachment (Perry, 1997). I wish I had had such knowledge to help me bond with our son.

The boy is lost

After I had asked him to do some chores, I waited for the boy to come back to the house, but he was nowhere to be found. His brother came back from outside, only to tell us that he heard his brother say he was going to go back to Uganda where he used to live because life was much better there. Did I hear this well - a mother who was excited that finally I was united with my son, only to be told that he might have taken off? Besides, we were still new in the city and where were we going to begin looking for him? We began to look for the child, calling and running around all the streets, but the boy could not be found. It took us about thirty minutes before we realized this boy did not even do what he had been asked to do.

In only one month, we did not know our son well enough to understand his personality. It was still too early to know what kind of a child he had become after over three years of not being with us. We were left with questions of how his aunt might have treated him. We were puzzled whether he was never asked to do even a simple house chore. The men in the house started questioning me whether I said anything that might have upset him. My answer was a definite "no".

After thirty minutes of panicking, his young brother found him hiding behind one of the house corners. When we asked him why he hid himself, he gave us no answer. We have never asked him since then. It was difficult to understand what this boy was trying to show us as parents. I am sure psychologists and counselors who work with abandoned children understand what this behavior demonstrates. Could it be that he was now attention seeking after a long time without being with his parents? May be he was hurt for being left behind? Could it be that he was fearful, confused or hungry for love? We have not opened this chapter in his life, but waiting for the right moment when he is finally ready to talk about his early childhood abandonment experience.

Of course there were moments of blaming ourselves about leaving this boy behind. However, we had to think back and begin taking a good and hard look at ourselves to identify things we were allowing to get in our way, in order to be better parents to all of the boys. We had to identify things that we would not want to see or entertain as negative thoughts, for example perhaps that someone else must have done something to this child when he was left behind. We never even wanted to look at the hardships we had faced. We took personal responsibility about what was happening to our son, and made a commitment to do whatever it took to make change even when it got uncomfortable to do so.

When people are faced with difficult situations, especially disappointments that seem to be worse than the previous ones, there is always a wish of wanting to go back to your old environment, thinking that it was much easier and more manageable than the current situation. Disappointment is one of the most common phenomena, which cause people to deeply become hurt. When we are hurt in our current situations, we always want to retreat to the former life as the last resort.

If expectations have been raised and then unfulfilled, or if promises were made and not kept, then our trust is breached and we are wounded in spirit (Meyer, 2008). I had given our son false hopes about the future, especially about joining his father. He found this was totally false. There were other aspects of our situation that did not resemble a better life, especially congregating in a suite, which was uncommon to this boy. We talked to him and educated him about the danger of hiding from his family and the emotional pain it brought to the family. Fortunately, we never saw any such behavior thereafter.

Joy filled with mixed feelings of loneliness

I had gone through a whole lot during and after the war in my country. I had been hit with sickness, poverty, psychological and emotional traumas. However, my spirit was still full of hope despite the ordeals of life I had experienced. What made this possible was my faith and the support of brethren sisters in faith I met and who were very supportive. Meyer (2008) argues:

> Even if we are sick, as long as our spirit is strong and healthy, we will be able to cope and keep going. But when we are damaged in our spirit, even the slightest problem, physical or otherwise, can crush us, causing us to lose control over our spirit. When this happens, we become defenseless and vulnerable (p. 7).

Life in Kinshasa was a mixture of joy and adventures. My excitement about coming to live in Kinshasa as a family unit came with a host of mixed emotions. After one month in the capital city, I was pregnant with our fourth son. It was an unexpected gift because our plans were focusing on getting out of Africa. I was faced with the language problem; the main language was French and Lingala, languages I hardly spoke. Language is a necessary tool that one cannot survive without in any given circumstance. It is needed for day today survival. Despite my family being of the same "ethnic" group of "African" people with the same features and skin color; language became a barrier for me to integrate in this new environment. I see this language problem associated with the process children use in acquiring first and second languages. I was totally lost, because learning the local language required meaningful interactions and practice.

Going for groceries was difficult for me. I depended on my husband or anyone who might be around to go with me if my husband was busy doing something else. I was the only woman in the whole house of 19 men. In the meantime, I became tired every day as the pregnancy progressed. I had my own illusion that coming to Kinshasa was going to be a smooth transition from rural area to city life. Instead I felt lonely. The fear of the unknown compounded with my being so far from friends and the support network I had developed while up country, caused all sorts of sicknesses that had no medical diagnoses.

Loneliness can be a gateway to other negative emotions. If we don't deal with it, we could end up also battling feelings of bitterness, anger and frustration. Each one of these has serious consequences (Stanley, 2008). I needed women to be around. There were times when I went and sat by the roadside to see if I could see anybody that spoke Swahili, a language that I had learnt from up country. This was a very naive idea, one might think. But wait until you hear what happened.

In this desperation, I came to realize that language is an important tool in human life. Language gives someone a sense of identity. Language connects a person and allows one to establish friendship, to express issues of concern, and to be able to maneuver ones' way in and out of situations. As Creese reminds us in Agnew (2007), quoting Norton (2000), she argues, "language is learned, communicated, and understood in the context of broader power relations" (p.358). With language difficulty, I was totally handicapped. How could I survive in a huge Capital City of 6 million people without any support network? I was also faced with the challenge of delivering my baby in an only male environment. I grew up in a culture where men were not expected to be around a woman when she was in labor. Unfortunately, none of these fears brought any solace to my anxieties.

It is not a good feeling to live controlled by fear. James (1987) explains:

> Fears can be transmitted before birth. Medical science has shown us that the infant in the mother's womb can pick up the fear and rejection of the mother...for some there is abandonment and rejection at birth that leaves fearful scars that can last a lifetime. As the negative can be transmitted, so can the good, the lovely, {and} the pure (p.92-93).

Despite trying to create a happy face for myself and forget about my own fears for the sake of my unborn baby, I still continued to have the anxieties of "what if the baby comes at night when there is no woman to call for help"?

Several medical publications show how rejection can damage the life of the unborn child. Rejection can also be a major culprit for causing a crushed spirit as Meyer (2008) reminds us. I did not want to crush my unborn child's spirit. I tried to amuse myself by making alliances with some of the men that lived in the house. On occasion, I would ask some of them to take me to the furthest market in the city where I could go and have some kind of fun. This strategy helped me forget about my personal turmoil. It helped and it worked!

As mentioned earlier, I looked for any alternative that would distract me from internal stimuli of thinking about my situation. I looked for therapy by sitting on the roadside. It was very therapeutic as it distracted me from thinking about the loneliness and isolation. The most interesting part with this therapy is that the capital city has all sorts of different types of women with different hairstyles, fashions and appearances. I saw women who knew how to dress up like they were going for business meetings or parties. The most amusing part was seeing women dressed up like they were going for job interviews, even on ordinary days.

In Africa, for a woman to be big or large, is a sign of beauty and pride. It shows how much a husband looks after his wife, or it is a sign of wealth. I fantasized being in their very situations and recalled my good old days when I used to be as happy as I saw these women. Unfortunately, I fitted none of their outward characteristics. In these cultures, people admire the outward look, especially the size as distinct from the west, where being large sometimes may be a sign of sickness. In Africa, many perceive large body size as a sign of beauty, prestige and success. In the Western cultures/societies, it would be considered obesity. Similarly, many parts of the African countries do not have any such definition of obesity or consider it as a disease as described by Renzaho (2004). Instead, in some parts of Africa, being overweight or obese is considered to be a sign of accomplishment, affluence, vigor and happiness for generations (Masinda & Kambere, 2008).

My husband tried to put me to the standards of these women by buying beautiful designer clothes, the clothes were worn by wives of diplomats. Surprisingly, each time I wanted to put on my dress, I looked like a scarecrow! I tried to mimic the way these women walked, but all was in vain. These city women were large with big bodies and beautiful! What could I do? Should I just try to get all my clothes and wrap them around myself to create a huge body? It was not easy trying to put myself into some image that was not mine. I tried to walk like them with a pretentious protruded bum, but all was not possible. I finally told myself, Edith, can you be yourself and stop mimicking someone else? Indeed, as I became myself with my slender body although pregnant, I managed to walk normally and happily.

I learnt one lesson out of this experience and that is, no matter what we try to be, one cannot be someone else and manage to do things that one would want to do. We can never be happy because we want to be someone else. A person can only be happy and manage to move on with life when you are your own self. Joyce Mayer (2002) points out, "I learned a long time ago that it does no good to try to get a person to be something he is not" (p.59). I was indeed miserable because of wanting to be some other identity when I could not create and be that identity.

Instability in the Capital City Kinshasa

Life continued to be challenging as we settled in the city. The population was not happy with President Mobutu Sese Seko's long stay in leadership. There were riots in the streets by people who were opposed to the leadership, and the local people joined the opposition for demonstration against his regime. Nonetheless, I was not ready for more fighting like what we had just escaped from Uganda. Each day that went by, the chaos intensified. There was much shooting, shouting and chanting. When my husband realized that I was faced with emotional torment, he connected me to a social worker and nurse who were working with the UNHCR office and spoke Swahili. They came to see me whenever they had time after work, for emotional support. At least I was able to talk with someone about some of the fears that I was facing. They assured me not to worry about my delivery or the delay that the baby might cause for our resettlement. This is what I really wanted to hear.

The assurance gave me some hope, which helped me move on the next day. As Osteen's (2005) words capture the essence of what I experienced, he writes

> Everywhere you look these days, you can see people who are hurting. Some people are extremely discouraged; many have broken dreams. Others have made mistakes, and now their lives are in a mess. They need to feel God's compassion and His unconditional love. They don't need somebody to judge and criticize them, or tell them what they're doing wrong. They need somebody to bring hope, somebody to bring healing, [and] somebody to show mercy. Really, they are looking for a friend, somebody who will be there to encourage them, who will take the time to listen to their story, and genuinely care (p.271).

I really needed someone to lift my spirit up. Yes, this social worker and this nurse had their own obligations to fulfill, but each time they came, I felt different. Sometimes they would come for prenatal care and/or to check on the refugees after there had been some demonstrations in the city. It was their obligation to ensure we were safe, since we were under UNHCR Geneva convention protection, and it made such a difference for me. By the look of things, I was coming from a hot pan of poverty and family separation, to what I will call the fire of political instability in the capital city of Kinshasa. The children were affected as well, seeing all the turmoil that was going on in the streets.

My three little boys learnt to pray each day. When you hear innocent children pray, you only shed tears because their prayers are surely genuine! Their prayers were, "God help mum to have a healthy baby; God, please stop these gunshots so that we don't die; God, please take us out of this country so that we could go to Canada and go and have a good life, study, and be happy." Wow! When a mother hears such prayers from innocent children what happens to her emotionally? Of course these innocent pleas really broke my heart, but I also got encouraged by their prayers because these were innocent children and I didn't know where they got these passionate and spiritual insightful words. Surely, they were inspired.

Children are often looked at as though they have little knowledge about their surroundings. Being with my three sons at the time taught me how children feel our pains when we hurt. It is the prayers of these innocent children that gave me the courage to move on for another day. I felt like someone who had a support network of people that was aware of what I was faced with. I came to realize that we should all be appreciative of what we have around us and not undervalue it. After all the ordeals of the riots in the streets, I finally found another female person during the demonstration period. The girl had just come by the house to check on the refugees in the Mason. I don't know what her role was, but I can only say she was doing some missionary- like work with the refugees in the Mason De-passage. I introduced myself to her and informed her of my loneliness.

She was waiting to be reunited with her boyfriend in Belgium. With this connection, I was not sure whether I should pour out my heart to her since she might be leaving the country soon or just keep to myself. Developing trust with new people can be challenging, especially if the person you are trying to do it with has not had similar challenges you have experienced. She was talking of joining her fiancée, which meant this girl had a good life if she could have someone living abroad. It was a matter of developing some rapport before I could even think of expounding on my emotional frustrations to this girl. She assured me that her family would support me by any means. I waited for over a month before I heard from her mother who she had assured me would visit.

After one month, the same girl showed up at the house and invited me to go with her for a prayer crusade. She told me that the person who was preaching spoke English and thought I would benefit from the crusade. It was joyful listening to the message that gave me hope and courage. I finally had the opportunity to hear someone preach in the language that I understand. However, the situation in the city continued to deteriorate with daily killings and shootings. Consequently, my husband arranged for us to run for safety with the children to this new girl's house. He suggested that he would stay behind, but at least save my life and that of the children. It was impossible for me to do this, but he persuaded me to go with the children for safety and that he would follow us later. I carried the third child on my back while the two other kids and I walked two miles to the girl's house. It was not safe for us to do so because, there were continuous shootings in the streets and beatings of anybody that was suspected to be pro-government.

Under such circumstances, we were only at the mercy of God, not sure that we would make it to our destination. My husband simply encouraged me to walk on. It was hard for him to see the whole family of five in this dangerous place with children crying and hiding under the beds. It was the norm, whenever there were gunshots. People hid under their beds. What a horrible experience!

My husband and I had to make a quick decision to get the children out of this hostile environment, and took refuge at the neighbor's place. My little boys were put on the frontline to guide me through the streets with mobs of hostile citizens, who were ready to rough-up anybody pro-government. This arrangement was due to lack of communication, where if I knew the language, I would have been the one holding the hands of my little boys. I was at their own mercy as we crossed the streets not knowing whether we would make it to the house where we were going. When we arrived at the house people were shocked to see us at their door. It was obvious we had risked our lives.

A few minutes after we left the Mason De-passage, it sounded like the battle was at our house. Is this what we expected to meet in the capital city, to be greeted by the cross-fire of bullets? Was everyone at the house safe? I feared that my husband and everyone in the house had been killed. I simply wanted to go back immediately, to go and die with my husband. I was bothered with questions from my children whether their dad was safe.

Suffice to note that when a person has gone through trauma, it is very difficult to want to go through any similar situation. I desperately wanted to simply go back and be with my husband. I believe the women in this house saw me as a sick woman who was psychiatrically not well. They ignored me any time I wanted them to explain to me what was going on. I did not want to hear anything, but to simply go back.

It was torture, especially being in a place where you cannot even speak or communicate with the local people! After three hours of heavy shooting, finally things calmed down. We went back to the house expecting the worst. As we approached the house, my heart started pounding, not knowing what to expect. We finally entered through the fence of the house and found everyone fine. We all rejoiced and thanked

God for taking us through the day, which was so much more horrible than any of the other days that we had seen during the demonstrations.

The UNHCR office sent one of their probation officers to come and check on us at the Mason De-passage. We were advised that when such demonstrations happen, no one is allowed to go outside the house because we were under the Geneva Convention and no one was supposed to touch us or even shoot at us. Was this true? Does a bullet have any discernment to kill its target? They were shocked to hear that I had dared to go out with the children and walked through the angry mob. In this chaotic situation, as time passed by, it looked like a hundred years. We continued to live under intense fear of Mobutu's regime for at least seven more months before we got resettled to Canada.

The power of social networking

Everywhere I went, I had to begin creating a support network, which was not easy. One evening I saw a woman come through the gate and asked for me. The woman told me of how she had heard that there was a woman who might be from North Kivu who spoke Kiswahili. She introduced herself as someone who spoke the language and that she was from Lubumbashi, a district in the DRC whose indigenous people speak this very language. This is what I had been longing for! I finally had someone who identified with me, but with her own problems as well. She was poor and had been estranged from her husband who left her for another woman. She was in as much need as I was. This is what I was used to; working with rural women. I was now in a position to extend my help to someone! As our friendship developed, I realized that she had been feeling lonely as well and needed someone to connect with and share her own frustrations.

The bond between us grew stronger and both of us felt we needed each other. Whenever I visited her I found that she was living in a very tiny house with her three children. In most of the African culture, women remain poor in all spheres of influence, especially if they have no education or resources to do business. Men are generally the breadwinners while women stay at home looking after the little ones. If a man is not in the picture, in most cases, some of the women, especially rural women, have to shoulder the burden of fending for the family.

This woman had no education, and of course with nothing to depend on to help her children. She depended on a small-scale business, which did not bring enough income for the family. She was more in need than I was. The fact that she came to look for a refugee woman who was lonely warranted me to give her due respect and attention that she needed. As Osteen points out:

> ...compassion in your heart toward someone, (is) offering you an opportunity to make a difference in that person's life. You must learn to follow that love. Don't ignore it. Act on it. Somebody needs what you have to give. Many people are unhappy and are not experiencing life to its fullest because they've closed their hearts to compassion. They are motivated by only what they want and what they think they need. They rarely do anything for anybody else unless they have an ulterior goal in mind. They are self-involved and self-centered" (ps. 272-273).

I realized that I also had something to give her more than what I got from her: friendship! I realized that my passion to help the poor was now coming into place. It had been years since I went out to help groups of women like her. I found fulfillment in doing what I did, helping her with shopping and cooking even though she did most of the talking when we went shopping. She was very appreciative, but I was more appreciative than she was because I found someone that I could socialize with. Omartian (2006) points out, "We can never be truly whole and fulfilled or find any lasting peace unless we are giving to others. We release the flow of God's blessing to us by letting them flow through us" (p. 218). Omartian further elaborates, "Let us not love in word or in tongue, but indeed and in truth" (p.220). Osteen (2005) also illustrates that:

> Sometimes if we would just take the time to listen to people, we could help initiate a healing process in their lives. So many people today have hurt and pain bottled up inside them. They have nobody they can talk to; they don't really trust anybody anymore. If you can open your heart of compassion and be that person's friend without judging or condemning and simply have an ear to listen, you may help lift that heavy burden. You don't have to know all the answers. You just need to care (p.273).

I needed someone to care for me, much as I came to learn that she needed someone too. We humans are social beings who need each other.

We only need to be there and listen to our fellow human beings and hear what their needs are. We need to be sensitive to what their real needs are and be able to help them. Money can help solve some of our problems, but even a million dollars cannot bring happiness when someone is isolated. It is the listening ear and people who show that they care and understand one's situation that matters most.

The UNHCR social worker and nurse who checked on us every so often did not come back any more. I only met them at the office whenever we had an appointment with them or had something that we wanted to pick up from their office. This never bothered me after all because, I had now developed my own social connections with the local women. As a professional social worker, I have seen the importance of connecting immigrant and refugee women with other local women whom they can identify with. Even though I may support them as a professional, there is always a gap that exists between us because I am perceived as the "other" due to my professional title. The support network they receive from their fellow local women brings a different perspective to their social life than that of a professional. Those professionals from the UNHCR had their own social network and social life, which I did not share. They might have spoken the language that I understood, but there was something that was different between us: professionalism and client relationship!

As a professional in the Western world, I now understand the nurse and social worker acted out of professionalism. It was not that they did not want to come and visit me, as I had needed. It would have been professionally unethical for them to develop a personal relationship with a client. Besides, they felt that the need was not so strong since I had my husband and children around to keep me company. The only aspect they forgot was isolation from a support network of other women, which was vital, especially being in a strange country with language limitations.

Child birth that connected old friendships

The story I present here is a miracle. It was an afternoon like any other. I was very pregnant and tired. Like any other day after lunch, I had had a nap while my children and husband were playing chess in the Mason De passage common room. In my deep sleep, I heard someone knocking at the door of our bedroom suite. It was one of the men that shared the house with us. He told me that there was someone outside looking for me. I got up and opened the door.

I was shocked to see one of my friends from up-country standing at the door. There was lamenting, shouting and laughing; I had not laughed for the last eight months since I came to live in the city. The whole house was chaotic. The men who were in their rooms came running to see what had happened. Others thought the baby had been delivered. It was chaos all over the house. My husband and children came running to see what had happened, only to find my friend Shelina and I dancing at the door. My husband joined the laughter; the children simply stood by watching the excitement unfold.

Shelina had been in the Capital City over six months to join her husband whom she had been estranged from for over seven years. She longed to see me, but did not know how to locate us in the city with six million people. It is very interesting how longing for a support network can all fall in place in an unexpected way. Shelina was the woman who had gone to get my son from Uganda. Our connection was a miracle after she had made several attempts to find us, but to no avail. It was the beginning of a support network that would finally bring some hope and mental fulfillment. Within a few days we were connected with another friend, "mama" Feza, whom I met in Goma as I was coming to Kinshasa. We connected, and she became an added strength for help for us as a family.

My experience reminds me of what I have been seeing with so many refugee women, children and families. I have realized that isolation can also cause a lot of emotional and psychological effects on an individual. Social connection is very therapeutic in many refugees' lives. What I have to mention here is that when I was pregnant with my third son, before relocating to Beni, the two women I am talking about here had supported me emotionally and spiritually; they had become like family. What had been a very strong connection and support network was being established in Kinshasa once again. Having both friends around was therapeutic. We were assured of support in case we had problems because there were people around to help us with the children.

A refugee woman in labor

On January 7, 1992, I had a high fever and was rushed to a refugee clinic. I was in my eighth month. Within a few minutes of being in the doctor's room, my water broke. This baby was not yet due because, I still had one more month before delivery. However, the baby simply wanted to push itself into the world. Moreover, this baby was going to be premature, and arrangements were made for me to be taken to a nearby hospital which had the equipment that would keep this child alive. I was placed on constant monitoring and observation by male student doctors, something I did not expect. With all my three boys, I had never been delivered by a male doctor. I simply wanted to run each time these young doctors came to monitor the condition of the baby. I had been in this constant monitoring situation for 4 days!

With the worry of limited experience of these young doctors, there was also the frustration of language. Communication was difficult for us because they did not speak Swahili; neither did I speak French, which was the only local language people spoke. The nurses and doctors were very frustrated by my inability to speak the local languages or French. They eventually learnt that I was a refugee from Uganda, waiting to go to Canada. Surprisingly, mentioning that I was going to Canada elevated my status. Some of the students tried to speak with me in the little English they had learnt at school. At least this brought some connections and friendship with these young doctors. In the initial stage of these doctors' assessment with me, there could have been someone who spoke at least a language that I spoke. However, this came about at a later stage as I will explain later.

I was in intensive care for three days because I was getting weaker with each hour that passed without any signs of the baby's delivery. I had no idea what was happening nor did I have anybody to ask about what plans they had should the contractions completely stop. Finally, one of my friends, Feza, came to stay with me and helped with communication. Agnew (2006) tells us that *"language is used to convey a set of meaning and since it provides a bridge between the social world and us, we need to know in any given context who is saying what and why they are saying it"* (p.6). I wondered what these doctors were saying to each other whenever there were consultations. Was the baby fine in the womb? What was the new development that these doctors could not share with me? All these were questions that had no answer because I was not able to even explain myself. I became the object and subject for all the male student doctors to do their experiments and studies they were conducting.

I come from a culture where I had never been to a gynecologist nor had I ever had such an experience; only in emergency situations, but for a few minutes, not three days of continuous monitoring. In my country, during my three sons' deliveries we used midwives. This invasive medical process was quite unusual to me and at the time, I felt it was a very humiliating process, to have my baby delivered by male doctors. I now know how different systems work differently. I am certain things have changed quite a lot even in the country where I grew up and delivered my other sons.

Traditionally, in the place where I grew up, it was always the elder women who stayed with a young woman who was in labor, to encourage her and support her in every way possible. In fact, traditional midwives play a major role in the health system of childbirth in the African cultures (Masinda & Kambere, 2008). In contrast, in Kinshasa, I found the nurses to be very proud and not cooperative. I am not sure whether they were frustrated by my inability to communicate in their local language. This is a question that never got answered. Eventually, after three days in the hospital, with no progress of the child coming, the nurses started whispering to each other; some would ask my friend whether she was aware that the baby had died in the womb.

Professional nurses are not supposed to discourage family members who are looking after a sick person, but when they started whispering to my friend that the baby inside was already dead, what did that mean to her psychologically? It was hard for her to believe these claims because she was consistently checking on me to find out about the baby's movement. Besides, my friend was a well-respected senior woman in taking care of pregnant women according to our African culture. To her, there was nothing alarming about this delay. She consistently asked me if everything was okay. I could not understand the relevance of her questioning, but later I learnt that the nurses had been misinforming her about the condition of the baby. Was it professionally right to be telling my friend news that would devastate her after all?

Finally, after a long wait, my husband was asked to sign consent forms, allowing the doctors to do a C-section. This meant us transferring me to another hospital, very expensive where diplomats were treated. Arrangements were made for us to get transported to this third hospital with emotional feelings about whether the baby was safe, seemingly confirming the nurses' predictions. He finally delivered the news to me after he had regained the courage to share news of relocating. He assured me that things were going to be okay and I needed not to worry. I had not expected to hear this news, to have a C-section.

In the Ngaliema Hospital

As I was lying in bed very exhausted and helpless, I saw my husband come with the student doctors who had been working with me. My husband spoke the local language, so communication was not an issue for him. There was transport waiting for me to another hospital. We drove to Ngaliema, a very prestigious hospital for diplomats, and arrived there late afternoon. At 3 PM, Monday, January 13, 1992, I was taken in the room with a male nurse who spoke Swahili. Finally it had been arranged for me to have someone with whom I could communicate. He introduced himself as someone who was preparing me for C-section. It did not matter to me being prepared for surgery by a male nurse. What mattered therapeutically for me, was finally having someone who could speak the language that I understood. Although I was emotionally exhausted, at least I was strengthened by having someone around with whom I could communicate. I had the courage to tell this nurse to first pray with me before I went into the theater, which he did. In my situation, as in many others, language cut boundaries and it was indeed very rewarding to know there were people who could understand what I said.

Language is healing and a connecting factor that bridges gaps. When I was taken in the theater, there was a young good-looking doctor, who also spoke Swahili! Before he started the C-section procedure, he engaged me in a conversation, asking when I would be traveling to Canada and in which province I was going to live. At that time, I had no idea. Further, he inquired about my previous deliveries and whether there were any difficulties. My husband further inquired whether I needed to continue having more children, and if my previous deliveries had been successful and easy. Keep in mind, in the African context, having more children is part of the culture. It is not a problem having many children because parenting is looked at as a community responsibility (Masinda & Kambere, 2008). Further, there are a lot of sicknesses that can kill children at any moment. Having few children means running the risk of having none or just a few should some of them die because of common diseases, such as malaria or cholera. In my case the last two children came unexpectedly since I did not have much knowledge about family planning. Besides, we were desperately looking for a baby girl! Having another baby boy was an added blessing; the only problem we were faced with was poverty and the continuous waiting period which lasted another year.

In the meantime, my husband was being tormented by the UNHCR to get us out of this hospital because it was very expensive. The UNHCR officers demanded that I get transferred to a local hospital where the conditions were affordable but deplorable. People slept on the floors because it was overcrowded. One woman explains the conditions that she saw there:

> There were so many troubles there because some time the mum dies and leave with one month or two months old and you just need to take care of them, to give milk to them, to feed them, they have some problems, some they got malaria, some they lose blood, so many problems around there, people die (Rose, focus group #1, Dec.2007).

One might even ask, what was their problem? Was it their money that they were worried about? This was UNHCR money from Geneva, which every refugee is entitled to receive! This is my story, but there are so many untold ugly stories that women face under such bureaucracies.

While I was in the theater, my husband was told that I had lost so much blood that I needed a transfusion. He was asked to donate his own blood to his wife, but unfortunately he did not have the same blood type. This was hard on him and the clock was ticking. He had to get someone to save my life. Where else and from whom could he get blood in this strange country when HIV/AIDS had become epidemic? As he was faced with the realities of being a stranger in a new society, a miracle happened and one of the boys that we lived with at the house had a blood test and had a match, he came to my rescue and volunteered to donate his blood. I will forever be grateful to this young lad, who later came to live in Canada.

Although this was a hospital for rich people and it had modern equipment, if you had a sick person who needed blood, the family members were obliged to buy their own blood to save their relative. And what about the HIV/AIDS problem? This is what my husband was faced with because it was going to be difficult for him to get someone to help him out within ten minutes in this heavily populated city as the hospital authority had demanded. This was the hand of God to bring this boy at the right time when we were at crossroads. My husband had been asked to provide two liters of blood and the boy could only provide one bottle. Amazingly, the doctors found one more bottle of blood in the hospital fridge, which they kindly agreed to give me on condition that my husband paid it back by donating his own blood to save someone else, which he did.

After the baby's delivery through C-section, we were faced with the fear of whether this blood was safe or whether it had been tested before they used it. We knew the life style of the young man who had donated his blood. But we knew nothing of the other donor. When one is faced with such a situation, one only depends on hope. We were hopeful that the people who had donated their blood were safe. Hope is a belief in a positive outcome related to events and circumstances in one's life.

Hope implies a certain amount of perseverance — i.e., believing that a positive outcome is possible even when there is some evidence to the contrary (Ammer, 1997). After this experience, we lived with fear, terrified for the worst. Each day that came by, we had to deliberately trust and hope that the blood was not contaminated with HIV/AIDS. We were constantly asking ourselves whether the boy was tested before they allowed him to donate blood. My husband was sure they did not because there had not been much time. The only thing he remembered was the person who took the blood from the boy, asked my husband if he knew the young man, and my husband said, "Yes."

Out of the hospital

We got out of the hospital after about a week. I healed fast, and the baby grew very big within four days of being out of the incubator. The hospital bill was 53 million Zaire which we were not worried about because that was UNHCR's responsibility to settle. This was a miracle. We saw the hand of God upon this child of eight months to survive without any complications.

One week later, my friend Feza was also hospitalized. My husband continued with the usual responsibility to care for our friend who had sacrificed so much by being with me in the hospital. Her experience was as painful as ours, but we both benefited from each other's pains. We learnt what it means by having someone who will continue to support you even in the hardest times. She stood by us just as we stood by her without jeopardizing our friendship. Sometimes we can find ourselves caught up in a web where we feel stuck, but there is hope that goes beyond measure. Ours is such that when we got out of the hospitals, there was something to celebrate; we were both alive and I had a healthy baby, who is now my joy.

After the baby had arrived, we were faced with the hurdle of reporting a new member in the family to an immigration officer in Abidjan, Ivory Coast. We were not sure whether this new member would delay the process of our resettlement in Canada. Amazingly the visas arrived two weeks after the baby was born. His name was included on the visa. This was a huge relief! The flip side to this was that the expiry date for the visas was May 23, 1992. We were again faced with the dilemma of getting the tickets for travel. On 18th May, the tickets arrived. The next day we were picked from our "Mansion De -passage", to go and get the required vaccinations for international travel. On May 20th we were given some travel money to buy all the necessary stuff, such as warm clothes for the children and a few bags to use to carry our belongings. The officer from the UNHCR who was assigned to help us do the shopping started lamenting about our expenditure. He was in charge of everything and decided what to purchase; if there was any money left after we purchased what we needed, it belonged to him. He advised us to not overspend so that he could save the money for himself.

The man informed us that coming to Canada meant that we would find everything laid for us on the streets. He informed us that everywhere one walks on the streets of the Western World, people simply pick up dollars without laboring for it. This is the information that most of the people come with as the women up country had initially told me when I went to join my husband. I recall hearing him say that he envied us, wishing that he were the one traveling to Canada because of the instability in Kinshasa. The place was in total chaos and every one wished to leave Congo because of this instability. This was the system that operated then and I believe there are still many more who take advantage of refugees. Can you imagine!

We left Congo on May 21 through Congo Brazzaville with a lot of mixed feelings. As is the case with many people, I do not take change with a good feeling. This relocation was going to be the fourth move since I left my home country, Uganda. I was not sure what kind of life and friendship I was going to again develop in another foreign country. Jaynes, S. (2004) states that, *"As you begin to move forward to accomplish your dreams, don't be surprised if you encounter a few border bullies of your own"* (p.229). I felt really exhausted from constantly making new friends, adventuring with new culture, new language and life styles.

Even after I had heard that there are greener pastures in Canada and an abundance of gold on the streets, this did not guarantee that I was going to find a friendly support network. At the same time, I was faced with the body image problem. I felt that my image figure was not comparable to the Canadian women's size. I needed to put on some weight before I traveled. There was fear that my husband would be laughed at for not looking after me. As I have said before, in Africa, being "fat" or "big" is a sign of wealth and beauty. To my amazement, I found that Canada had a different perspective about figure size. Can you imagine how different cultures perceive different body images in different ways?

I recall some of the boys I lived with telling me after reading Canadian news magazines about body images. They constantly informed me how in Canada being "fat" is a "disease" or an insult. It was hard to believe how this mentality resonated in the West. Did I hear these boys well or did I not want to take their words? I thought these were simply fabricated stories that they were creating. I felt that they simply wanted to make me feel bad about my tiny body size. This was the perception that I came to Canada with. After fearing whether we would make it to Canada on time before the expiry date of our visas, we finally landed in Toronto on May 23rd at 22hrs, just 2hrs before our visas expired.

After two hours, we were connected to Vancouver via domestic travel. What a relief that nothing was going to stop us from being in this beautiful place! My husband declared $5 US dollars on our immigration paper as money he had brought with him as he entered Canada. It was a requirement that everyone who enters the country declares whatever they brought into the new country. This money came with amazing blessings. As I write this book, it was remote in my mind that I would ever think of writing these words without tears of pain. I am so thankful that I can put these lines on paper to help anyone who has just come into the country without even five dollars to remain strong as long as they still have air to breathe, that the sky is the limit and nothing is impossible if you remain positive and focused. There is hope if you do not want your dreams to be shattered by your fears or past memories. Work on them and you will find one of many pathways that will lead you to more than you ever dreamt.

A New Horizon: From Africa to Canada

❧

> *All began on the night of May 23, 1992*

It is well documented that once refugees settle in a host country, new belief systems, values- and more challenge their adjustment. Families may be disrupted once again by new family roles and patterns. During the resettlement process, many refugee women re-establish their lives and encounter Western systems such as Mental Health services for the first time (Masinda & Kambere, 2008; Rousseau, 1995). To the new immigrant woman in Canada, resettlement means loss of homeland, family, friends, and material possessions, and the challenges of a new language and culture upon arrival. However, Osteen (2005) has something to say to these circumstances,

> Even when circumstances don't go your way, keep your mind set in the right direction. If you do your part by continually contemplating the goodness…living with the faith and expectancy [faith] will take you places you've never even dreamed of, and you'll live at a level you have never before dared to imagine (p.28).

We have all gone through times when we felt our spirit was wounded, but healing can also come through the same testing times when you remain positive and keep a positive attitude, you stand to gain. Given the trials that many refugee women endure before arriving at their new destinations. These trials do not mean that they will not face even worse ones. However, they become a catalyst that helps them go through new hurdles as presented in the following chapter.

On the night of May 23, 1992, after arriving at the Immigration Services Society of British Columbia, a non-profit society helping newcomers to settle in Canada, my little boys were very excited and so was my husband. I was the only woman in the group and I had ambiguous feelings about this new adventure. These five men had something to celebrate. The boys finally connected with their father because the environment was safe for rejoicing. They all loved playing chess games with their dad- a game that I totally resented with a passion because each time they played, I totally felt left out. I had not learnt how to play it and neither did I want to try. After the chess game, my husband and I could walk around the streets where we lived, to go for groceries. Everything looked so strange, but at the same time beautiful. Of significance were down town clean streets, which were well lit, with tall buildings with magnificent window glasses.

One evening, we were about to go to bed. Through our bedroom window, I saw some sparkling lights and heard some sounds that sounded like gunshots. Oh, the expression on my face! You should have been there to see how I started jumping up and down trying to hide myself under the bed, screaming that I was again in danger of war. My husband and our two eldest sons took a close look to see if truly what I saw were bullets flying in the air. They saw nothing of the sort. I started lamenting, "What is this that I have again come to face? Here I am running from trouble, but the same trouble has followed me in the white man's land?" My husband tried to calm me down, but my heart was racing like a rocket. It was obvious that I had started re-living the past memories.

These blasts and bright lightings went on for at least five minutes before they subsided. Could it be true that these were not gunshots as my husband had explained? My boys were not even bothered with what I was facing. They only enjoyed watching the flashes in the air. I was not sure what really convinced my little boys that they were not gunshots when they had just come from a situation where they witnessed gunshots. Could it be that children forget so easily? To me, in this one week our land of opportunity seemed to have turned into a danger zone.

Eventually it was time to go to bed- but my heart was not at peace. I could not get any sleep whatsoever. I started questioning my husband whether it might be possible that the Government we were running from had now heard of our relocation to Canada. The question my husband asked me was, "Who are we that a whole government would send its army to come and shoot us in the developed world"? Before he finished the sentence, all the five men in the house were totally asleep snoring before I even closed my eyes. They were not bothered by what we had just witnessed- *"a fireworks display!"*

It was still very difficult for me to believe or trust my husband who could not understand the emotional and psychological torment I was going through. I kept reminding him of the torment I went through when the thugs came and started chanting at my house wanting to kill him after the government had been overthrown. None of what I told my husband made sense to him. I got furious with my little boys, thinking that I would get sympathy from them. After seeing all that I had just gone through, how could these children simply get to sleep and start snoring immediately without keeping an eye on me? What in the world was going on in these little kids' heads to leave their mother tormented by these fireworks as they later called them?

Is it a common practice when someone has had troubles or past negative experiences they will always look for sympathy from innocent children who do not understand the nature of the situation? I am not a psychologist, but this is what I have looked back at and wondered about. My husband asked me, "Who in their own mind would say, this family has gone to Canada, let us look for all the ammunitions in the world to finish them off? Besides, what crime had we committed in Uganda that would cause a whole government to come and look for us in Canada?" he asked. However, nothing that my husband told me convinced me at all or made sense to me, because I was deeply trapped in my own world of re-traumatization.

For the whole night, I rehearsed my past pains. I was particularly angry at my little children who could not wait to see what would unfold of these fireworks. More disappointing for me was the way they snored when I was busy re-living my past. It may sound very ungracious for a mother to get so disappointed with innocent children who literally knew nothing about my past, but that is where I was at during those days. Osteen (2007) explains some of the important aspects of letting go of the past and embracing ones' future. He points out that:

> You have to let go of your disappointments, let go of your failures, and let those doors totally close behind you. Step forward, into the future that God has for you, knowing there's nothing you can do about past disappointments. You cannot change the past, but you can do something about the future. What's in front of you is far more important than what is behind you. Where you are going is more significant than where you came from or where you have been. If you have the right attitude, you will give birth to more in

the future than you've lose in the past. Quit looking back. This is a new day" (p.19).

However, I was not there yet. I had a lot of baggage to sort through. I do not think that I had one recollection that would have brought me to my normal self, especially when I knew that I had the right to be fearful of these fireworks. It was very difficult for me to envision a new day after coming from such a horrific experience of war trauma. I was faced with the uncertainty about the new social, emotional and economic challenges. It was another chapter in my life. Finding my identity and fitting in a society where I was being questioned about my new identity of being an immigrant woman. For instance, I was constantly asked, "By the way, where are you from? Your accent is different, I can't understand what you are saying!"

On that May 25, 1992, we were new Canadian immigrants with my husband and our little four boys, ages 8, 7, 2 1/2 and a 5 month-old baby. Everywhere I went I was called by my new "status" of an immigrant African woman. It was a dream come true despite the status because, this is what my husband and I had envisioned in 1985 while running away from the repressive regime of military dictators, to work and live in a land of freedom and peace. However, we did not know how life was going to unfold as we started discovering everything that our new home in Canada was going to offer us.

The first challenge was looking for accommodation. There were six of us and getting accommodation was the most challenging task. No one wanted to accept a family with four little kids; besides, we did not have credit that would prove us to be people of good economic standing. Each time we were asked where we worked and our responses were enough for the landlords to simply close the doors on us. We had no good credit rating. If one comes to think about it, where could we have gotten good credit rating when we were simply new immigrants in the country? What else could we have done in such an instance where one is accepted to rent from someone by the position you have or credit history that you have? Besides, we were immigrants who did not have any credit rating before we came to Canada. How could we have a credit history when we were just new in the country? Is this what was expected of every new family that arrived in Canada? Apparently this is what our new society expected of us twenty four years ago, and many families still experience this to today.

Since that time, I have learned many lessons through my experience working with people from all walks of life. We all have our own baggage and stories that need a listening ear. Our stories are full of challenges, courage, and determination. Our stories are those of trauma and torture. None of us came to Canada having acquired any Canadian experience as we journeyed from country to country. We never acquired any university or college education along the way, but only hardships of waiting and sometimes, rejections after several attempts of doing interviews to be resettled in Canada. We did not come with any computer skills or good command of the English language as we went through the valleys and hills of challenges before reaching our final destination, and yet, when we arrived in Canada, these are the expectations.

These are some of the challenges that many refugee women encounter as they run from their own hardships which are not of their own making. Like many women, on my journey of finding meaning in life; the feelings of solidarity and a woman's strength are the motivations behind sharing of my own personal experience. We all have found courage and hope in each of our sharing.

For us immigrant women, to return to love, to work, and to play, knowing and trusting people; that is the task of resettling. Psychological and emotional turmoil from the task of being an immigrant who leaves their origins behind while not having fully settled in the new place, is not easy to bear. Getting caught in the middle, in its early phases identifiable as culture shock, in its later phases hardly ever identified, is a painful experience that doesn't really have an endpoint to us immigrants who come from war atrocities. Writing these concepts on trauma does not mean that I am an expert in counseling refugees from war troubled countries. I can only say that I am an expert in my own experience of being a victim of pre-post-migration pains. I am an expert in it because I lived it and have managed to be where I am, thus making me an expert in my own survival techniques.

Post-migration life experience and past memories

On July 15, 2008, I attended a conference and this is what one presenter said about re-traumatisation:

> Hurts and feelings that have been repressed are virtually immortal; after the passage of decades they behave as though

they had just occurred. Problems don't go away. They must be worked through or they remain. If you don't resolve your trauma(s), you continue to live with them and to repeat them (Dr. Adele Diamond's presentation, 2008).

Numerous publications confirm that memories of painful events can be selectively forgotten and later recovered (Herman, 1997). When I left Uganda, I thought this was the beginning of a new joyous life, thus leaving the old memories behind and starting a new life that was going to be glamorous. I did not know that this was going to be a continuation of trauma from Uganda to Congo, and then Canada, which would lead me to a long excursion that would develop into an interest in the topic of "traumatic experiences- pre and post- migration among refugee women." Through my work with local women, immigrants and refugee women, I have realized that my experience is not uncommon. Many women like me have suffered a lot of "depression" as a result of experiences only known to them. Let me shed some light here about the effects of depression, which affect almost a staggering 19 million adults and approximately 3% of children and 8% of adolescents in the United States alone (Mayer, 2008). When you have had past depressive experiences, if not dealt with at an early state, it will continue to surface by any trigger of such memories that resemble one's past experience.

Depression is so painful that it has a direct impact on your physical wellbeing. Depression makes people vulnerable to infections, and poor healing. It is scientifically proven that an individual who has had past depression tends to have generally poor health habits, which will most likely place them at even a higher risk of developing most types of disease (Herman, 1997; Masinda & Kambere, 2008; Miller, 2008). People who have had some depression as a result of displacement or any type of traumatic events are prone to poor nutrition, lack of exercise, use of alcohol and drugs, or overuse of prescription of medications (Mayer, 2008; Davis, 2006). Most of the women I have met during my work on this book, and many literatures that have been written about different people who have been traumatized have a common mechanism of dealing with their depression; using prescription drugs in order to get some sleep or be able to function normally.

In the case of my early years in Canada, I constantly had poor sleep patterns, which caused fatigue every morning I woke up. I could not go to sleep without taking sleeping pills, which in the end had some reactions on my body. I never wanted to do anything during the day because, I had no energy to do anything. I constantly had headaches that did not allowed me to function well to care for myself. This is a common pattern that many women from war trauma have shared with me. I have heard stories of women not coping well with daily activities without taking some kind of prescriptions because of fatigue or headache (Haskell, 2001). While acknowledging that the women participants for this narrative went through hardships, they were constantly faced with situations of depressions as a result of lack of support. Like many immigrants in Canada, here is what one woman explains as her experience during her integration period:

> You become useless to yourself. You have constant headaches. I have developed a tendency to forget even simple appointments due to stress. I have been so restless, pain in my whole body. Sometimes I go to the kitchen, but find myself in the bathroom. So these problems have been so prevalent of our lives. We are given medicine, which temporarily controls the problems so that I can forget myself...I think that maybe if someone died, I would not be going through all this [PTSD], which is very stressful and I become forgetful... One day my children even called an ambulance after I failed to wake up. I took 6 sleeping pills (Nina, Focus group #2, 2008).

From this explanation, it can be seen that women's celebration of their arrival in the new peaceful country is welcomed with mixed feelings of joy or depression. These feelings are in most cases the result of the illusions about the new home. Some of them come from the long waiting period about their refugee status, in order to have papers allowing them to work; then be able to save money and establish themselves. This becomes a period where most of us either quit and jump off the scale and grab something that is not really what we should be focusing on, a sense of regret, and then doing odd jobs that do not have any benefits. Some even forget that they have qualifications that could be up-graded and do something meaningful with them.

In each of the individual women's lives, the waiting to get legal status or getting family members they left behind in refugee camps to join them is the most testing of times. "My family is broken" was a headline in the Now Community Newspaper November 12, 2015 of a Somali refugee woman who left a four weeks old baby in a refugee camp in Kenya in 2009. To date the untold story of this immigrant woman is that of a broken family that has incubated an abated stress and depression in this woman's family. You wait for the unknown, you wait for the expected or wait for a long waited dream to come to pass, and yet, sometimes the waiting may come with unexpected problems that we all do not want to go through. In all these, none of the waiting comes without frustrations, challenges, or pessimism. It is a time when one might get discouraged or decide to call it quits, and have feelings of wanting to go back to the ugly circumstances that they left behind, as I felt in my first year in Canada.

In my case, the first two years were challenging as it was when I left my home country. Most of the time after the kids had gone to school I would spend my time sleeping on the couch thinking about so many things that had gone wrong in my life. This was a dangerous thing to do. Osteen (2005:21) has this to say,

> Remember, your actions will follow your expectations. Low expectations will trap you in mediocrity; high expectations will motivate you and propel you to move forward in life. But raising your level of expectations is not a passive process. You must actively think positive thoughts of victory, thoughts of abundance, and thoughts of favor, thoughts of hope; good, pure, and excellent thoughts.

Indeed, with strong support network from my landlady, some community family friends and a cluster of people whom I had built around me and believed in my strength, helped me to make it to the next level of my aspirations as you will read in the next chapters.

Reconnecting with my cultural roots

After living in Canada for many years and having adopted it as my second home, I decided to travel to Uganda to reconnect to my roots. In my journey of being a woman, mother and a professional social worker, I have learnt not to quickly release my negative emotions because people have made their own assumptions about me, something that will make me get stuck in my negative emotions. Writing these words has become one therapeutic way of releasing all my experiences while trying to see if these experiences could help other women who share similar cultures like mine, of being a woman, and also those who come from cultures similar to where I grew up.

In his book, *How to Get What You Want and Want What You Have,"* Gray (1999) demonstrates how pretending that you are in the past and processing your feelings by giving yourself the ability to feel, identify, and express your feelings can be an easy way to quicken the present healing. He says:

> When this is the case, the best way to process is to link what you feel now to something you felt then. The past is always easier to process. If we are afraid now, we don't know what the outcome will be. When we look back to the past, we can always reassure ourselves that things have and will work out. Even if we couldn't get the support we needed in the past, we can imagine ourselves getting that support. In this way, we can heal the wounds of the past (p.142).

Sometimes it is very difficult to get enough perspective from our pain and to feel it and let go, especially if we feel we have the right to be angry. Through my experience as an adult, I have found that living in the past can be dreadful. Rather, moving on and sharing my experience with other women to see how this could be a healing process for them means I have not allowed my past to shatter my dreams. I write this book to encourage anyone that has painful past experiences and dreams to not despair, but to keep working on those pains with the support of trustworthy friends and professionals and also to learn to let go and focus on your dreams. It is not easy, but I guess it is a process that we all continue to learn.

In September 2006, I found myself on a plane headed for Uganda, a country where I was born and raised. After 20 years in exile, I had not landed foot on the soil of this country. But this time around I made this trip with a group of volunteers from a support network that my husband and I had built since we arrived in Canada in 1992. The plan to go back to my home country started in 2004 after my husband and I completed a six-bedroom building where we wanted to start a school; we had land that had been desolate for over 17 years since we went into exile. I had vowed never again to set foot on the soil of my country, Uganda due to my previous traumatic experiences I encountered in that country. After a long deliberation about a trip to Uganda, I accepted to go back as my husband had suggested and see how we could revisit our old plan of building a school. Coming full circle I made a decision that the past cannot drive my future. I had not let go of my anger, emotional pain, and hatred for what I experienced when I was in that country. All sorts of emotions were playing on my mind as I counted down the time before the plane would land. I had a lot of mixed feelings about what to expect; I expected rejection, resentment and even hostility. Why did I expect all this? Because, the circumstances under which I left the country were precarious. It had been quite a long time without knowing what the situation I left was like, and on top of that, I had no idea how the people there lived after all these long years. Besides, I continued to carry the memories of hostility that I experienced when I was still in the country. There were feelings of love and empathy as I planned this journey because I knew in my conscience that what we were going to do was for a genuinely good cause. The reservations I had about my own country were based on my past experience, looking back at the conditions under which I left the country.

The group of 16 volunteers knew that we had wanted to build a school 20 years before, and the plan was being revisited 20 years later. As I sat on the plane, I experienced all the emotions of that time when my husband and I left the country. There were times on the plane where inwardly I cried out to God to spare my skin when we arrived in the country. I prayed, "Please God help me find a welcoming community." I kept on envisioning how people would receive me. There were fears of how people would treat me since it had already been a long time.

In my own imaginations, I felt that this burden of releasing feelings of the past experience was unbearable. I left the country with all this pain of being mistreated, when I felt we were innocent victims who tried to do the best we could for our people. We were only young people who were trying to do the best for our country and community, but found ourselves imprisoned and scornfully looked at by the very people that we served with pure hearts. How could I take that anger out of me as I was sitting on this plane? Crying to God gave me solace and a forgiving heart in order to ground myself in this community that I felt had betrayed me. But these questions and feelings were about to get erased as we continued with our journey. Yes, I found solace and peace as we sat on that plane for 16 hours. At the airport, I simply asked my God to save my skin from anything worse. Nobody in the group knew I was emotionally struggling. If I showed any feelings, this would have brought some mixed feelings to the team; I had to compose myself with dignity.

At 5:30 am, East African standard time, we arrived at the airport on that September 24, 2006, exactly 20 years after my husband and I had wanted to start a community school that would give the disadvantaged kids access to education. As the plane touched down, I recall one of the group members asking me, "Where are the airport lights? Are there no lights here in Uganda?" I had nothing to say because it was about twenty years since I had left the country. I was as unaware as she was. We finally landed and were directed to the immigration office. I was the only African woman and they called me "Mama Africa." These Westerners are always called "*muzungu*" in our Swahili language, meaning white person. So we kept those nick names as we identified each other. What a relief this brought to this *Mama Africa*! I had feared the worst. What if I was asked what I was doing in this group of people? What if they questioned why I left the country? What made me go and live in Canada? All these were questions that raced through my little mind, brimful of naivety.

Eventually, when the person that was guiding us to the immigration office saw that the crowd was too big to take one person at a time for declaration, he asked us to go and wait in one of the corners of the waiting room. What he did, which I felt was the wisest thing anybody could, was to request a leader from this group of Canadians to take the group's passports. Finally we were cleared by the immigration officers. The first person I met at the airport was my brother. I had kept the trip secret from everybody else because of fear of the unknown. From the airport we travelled to Western Uganda, where the Rwentutu school project is based.

Many places reminded me of my past. In her book, Marta (2003) demonstrates how sometimes our past adversities can bring healing to our present situations. She highlights that "Adversity used wisely strengthens self-confidence and instills courage" (p.276). The many years I spent with rural women, school children and now immigrant families have changed my perception as a person, mother, and professional. These experiences have changed me to refocus and value other people and about what I need to do with my life to help others.

After the overthrow of the government that my husband worked for, everything changed. My time with rural women, teaching and my role as a Member of Parliament's wife drastically changed. The time I had with so many visitors in my house was no longer there-time to cuddle our first born son, watch movies with my guests, or drive around with my son for fun were no more. I remained in an emotional haze for nearly two years after the government had been overthrown. I cried, but tears could not bring any solace to my then broken heart. As days turned into weeks, weeks into months, and months into years, my husband and I felt that we needed to start something that we would call our own-build a school where we would be the masters of everything.

This idea came up as a result of our frustration, anger and disappointment with the government that had overthrown the democratic government where my husband served. We felt that starting our own school would provide an opportunity for the rural children and would empower them to discuss their feelings about the poverty that had hit the country then. Not knowing what else we could do, how to acquire land to build the school, we turned to our own land of about forty acres. The motive was right, but the desire to want to show those who had hurt us and put us down was not right. God had a different plan. It would take twenty years for it finally to start.

Our journey to Kasese in Western Uganda was a six hour drive from Entebbe Airport. Kasese is the place where the project we went to visit is based. As we approached my own home district and a place that was part of my husband's constituency, I started crying out and yelling in prayer. The group of volunteers did not understand what I was going through and the trauma related emotions that were going on inside of me. We reached one place where our friend, had helped me run to safety, from the new government soldiers in 1985. As memories flashed back in my mind, I called out in prayers not being mindful that there were other people traveling with me in the car. I simply did not want those past memories and emotions to overcrowd my mind and the only way I could help myself out of this, was to cry out in prayers. From a clinical perspective, these were flashbacks of my past traumatic experiences and the only way I was able to cover up those thoughts was to cry out in prayers!

To my amazement, as we approached the place, only a few meters from where I had started screaming, I saw a group of traffic control police men in their uniform standing by their traffic car. Oh my, I wish you could have been there to see how my brown face instantaneously turned red. The first reaction was, "What in the world am I again into!" Ugly memories were almost making me faint. I composed myself without showing the guests that I was in such a panic. We were stopped; of course I had stopped praying, and only expected the worst; probably another slap similar to what happened to my friend twenty years ago. It had been about 15 years since I last saw a soldier carrying a gun. So what could I say since my nightmares had again become a reality?

This very place was in an area I used to be driven around as a Member of Parliament's wife, but here I was terrified due to what happened to me twenty years ago. To my bewilderment, I saw a different behavior of these men. They greeted us with respect and asked us where we were going. Of course we explained to them how we were volunteers visiting the area at a project in Rwentutu. Within minutes we were on our way to the project area, which was about twenty minutes away.

As the feelings of past memories bombarded my mind, I came to agree with what den Velde et al. (2000) in David Kinzie J, (2006) highlight regarding past trauma. Their contention is that, "Those [people] who were exposed to more severe war trauma were more common in the immigrant group... [they] suggest that severe stress from past war experience-not migration-was the major factor in the development of Posttraumatic stress disorder (PTSD)" (p.580). This is explicit that even following twenty years after I had gone through the trauma, the memories were still present.

The team that I was with had already shown some sympathy, not because they knew what I was going through, but because of the period I had spent abroad without seeing some of my relatives, and in particular, without setting foot in my home country. However, that was not the case. Mine was totally different. In fact, it truly was the past war trauma, and the re-invoking of those war trauma memories as I saw symbols of what I witnessed the night of July 26, 1986. Although there were challenges of how and what we were going to experience as we revisit our old dream, having people who are very supportive was equally important for my husband and I to meet our dream. Helping the vulnerable and poor community was our main dream, and this came to be fulfilled after twenty years.

As part of my African heritage, I grew up not knowing what volunteer work meant. The volunteer workers I went with were very determined to go to the community and do what had attracted them to Uganda. They wanted to be part of my dream, so dormant for such a long time. The power of this unforgotten dream to build a community school that would serve the Rwentutu children had been so strong that it helped me overcome the hurt, the anger, the resentment, the fear, and the hatred for my people, something that I had been holding on to for twenty years. To my relief, the situation in Uganda was totally different from what I had expected. We arrived at the project in Rwentutu, Kasese district, and we found a humble and welcoming audience of women and relatives that I had worked with during those early good days before the war, ready to receive me as their own daughter. They were excited to see us. As we worked together on the project, digging the foundation of the school building, the power and strength of my dream was present.

I really shake my head and marvel now that I can be able to write this story without any feelings of anger. As I share this story with many millions of women survivors of trauma, abuse, racial discrimination and professionals working with this population, I feel privileged to look back and see how my past traumatic experience can be a stepping stone to help me get the strength to continue with my life. I want to walk with you to help you understand how you can realize your dream.

Building Rwentutu community school and the women's micro-credit project have only become a reality because people have walked with my husband and I on our journey for this project, and when there were no people, God walked with us and carried us through for this project to come to fruition. With my own agony where I almost fainted, other women shared their own stories that became a mechanism for me to continue dreaming big. Obviously, writing this book, I was not isolated, as I did realize the importance of being connected with the people I had come to value as friends and acquaintances.

The community of Rwentutu inspired me even more because, when we have people who believe in what we dream, we can use the support to do things, not for selfish motives, but for the sake of those who need to be uplifted. Consequently, when on the journeys on which we find ourselves, no matter how painful our loads may be, we find that they become lighter, and the work fruitful. My experience of being a woman along with the stories of other women inspired me to walk this life of courage. At Rwentutu, I saw an outpouring of love from the community. Men, women, and children of all ages came to receive us as a group. There were tears of joy and excitement as people shared their joy for this project, in a community that was so deserted and isolated from all amenities in the district. There were words of encouragement from the local leaders, especially thanking my husband and I for not only looking at ourselves as now Canadians, but as people who still had faith in the people we had served earlier and left behind.

Parents were jubilant to see that a school was being built in their community where their daughters and sons would get an education without traveling miles across rivers. These rivers were known to even sweep people away, especially during rainy seasons where rivers usually flooded because of mudslides from the mountains. I recall one local leader, whose children also go to Rwentutu community school, who stood up in a crowd of many people that had come to greet us. His words to the group of volunteers were, "It is better for your son/daughter to go to unknown places than losing life." He further said, "If life had been lost as a result of war, we would not have had the opportunity of seeing a white man come to our land and help us develop this land with projects such as the ones you are planning for this community."

These words were meaningful to me personally. In his narrative, he expressed the joy that this community of Rwentutu had as a result of our group's visit. He asked them to send more volunteers to go and help with the project. I was struck by his words, showing the community's genuine attitude towards the guests. The anger I had had for the community and the entire country vanished, I came back from Uganda changed from hatred to love and empathy.

Sharing narratives from other African Immigrant Women

Here, my focus is on stories from other AIR women. My discussion relates to the women's experiences of not knowing where they belong after settling in their new countries.

Race matters

It is well documented that many clinicians and researchers do not routinely inquire about possible exposure to race related stressors, such as racial discrimination or assault that occurs solely or primarily because of the client's racial status or appearance (Scurfield, 2001). As one woman puts it:

I came from a troubled country. I thought I would find things much smoother. I found myself locked inside my house. I did not trust anybody that I met on the street…the cost of living is way too high. We are only given very little money to survive on. This makes me bleed inside my heart. I was confused about what to do… When the worker at Umoja African family Services

Center came to me, I said, finally I have found someone from my community. She started telling me about how to go about things. I was at least comfortable that I had a person who could give me information about things. Now if I want to cry, I will find other women who will cry with me because they have been in similar situations like mine (Kambere: group discussion; Feb.4/14).

Another woman laments:

Do you know what, when I come here at Umoja and I go without laughing, I don't feel well. But when I come here and you people make me laugh after talking about our issues, I feel this is very therapeutic (field notes: Kabira, June 2014).

The above comments demonstrate the importance of social networking with people who understand you and can make even a small joke that would stir your heart. It is the network of other women sharing their own survival experience that makes some of these women face another day with a smile. If you can get people to talk or write about their problems, their psychological and physical health improves. Talking or writing about previously inhibited experiences and translating them into language helps. Once it is language-based, people can better understand the experience and ultimately put it behind them. Translating a phenomenon into language alters the way it is represented and understood in our mind and our brain (Pennebaker, 2008).

Ultimately the task at hand is to recognize these women as producers of knowledge. Only at this level can we understand the extent to which socioeconomic forces are implicated in their suffering. At a deeper level, we must converse with the women in a *"dialogical model"* and not speak with them in *"appropriate mode"* (Dossa, 2004: p.4-5). This is what one woman reveals as her personal experience from both colleagues and employers:

I was the only black girl there. So they told the manager that oh she is not doing the job well. And the manager would see me busy doing my job well. And the manager said, oh Monna you are not ready, you are not accepted by other ethnic fellow refugee women at work. And now my four months being accused of not doing the job well, and the supervisor saying I am not doing a good job and being told you are going to be fired... but I asked myself how can I be fired within the four months of working for you? I have been here training people who came after me who did not know the job. Unfortunately without knowing, they brought me people to train them for my job. I was fired for no reason, nothing they said, but only to say you have to go because you are not doing your job. I said I don't know my job, you people you gave me the people to train. And I trained them. That day they gave me my papers, I came I sat there, and cried in my living room. I told my husband and said, this...I have to go and confront them... Even if you work hard, they won't accept you if they have already made up their opinion about you. You will work hard because of your color (Yvonne: focus group #1, Dec.2008).

It is clear from the women's social experience of migration that is embedded in their stories of survival and resilience that dealing with the Canadian harsh conditions of integration is not a smooth transition. When these women left their countries of origin, they were productive members of their societies, women of status and very knowledgeable. They were forced to live in refugee camps, in environments that they were not familiar with. Some of them had beautiful dreams that were shattered as a result of displacement. When they finally get resettled, they are given false hope about their future. What they struggle with is not closer to what they were told by overseas embassies.

Housing obstructions

In my case, when we arrived as a family of six, accommodation was a major challenge. Not only was it a challenge for me then, it continues to be a challenge for everyone. One woman describes her experience as she arrived in Vancouver:

My first year in Canada... when I got into the country, you are a new immigrant ...you know nothing, you expect people to tell you what to do and my first thing that bothered me most was accommodation. I went to the Inland Refugee Society they said they can only offer me accommodation for a week that was with the YMCA hotel. After that I was to look for my accommodation. I had to go where there was shelter, but I didn't know what... it was scaring me that people who were living there were all single men sharing with some women who had their own ways of doing things. To me it was totally different, it changed me. All my days in the first place was crying with nobody to help me out (Christina: focus group, 2004).

After getting a two-bedroom basement, we were faced with the challenge of falling sick every now and then. My boys shared one bedroom; three of them shared one bunk bed. Again, the same slogan of a shared bed as was the case in Kinshasa! My husband and I shared another room with our baby who was only five months then. It was apparent that when one of the family members fell sick, we all felt sick. In Congo, I lived in a refugee transition kind of house, where the six of us shared a suite, the same lifestyle continued in the developed world. Unfortunately this is not what I had expected. Why did we have to go through this? Later on, I realized that people never wanted to rent their places to tenants who did not have credit history or those who were on welfare. I really questioned myself where landlords expected people like us to have gotten these requirements when we were brand new immigrants?

Even getting this place was challenging, if it was not because of our Canadian host who helped us get this two-bedroom basement. Each time my husband called places, the person on the other end of the phone line would say, "I can't hear you; I can't understand your English accent. What are you saying?" Those who understood him asked him if he had a job. The moment he said, "I am on government assistance" the person simply hung up on him. As Creese argues:

Black African women in Vancouver live the legacy of British imperialism on many fronts, but nowhere more clearly than in their struggle to be recognized as competent speakers of English. Denigration of 'African English' accents recounted as a daily occurrence, cited in the failure to get access to jobs, promotions, rental houses, adequate services...and experienced through the daily correcting of pronunciation that friends, co-workers, and strangers alike seem to feel entitled to (Agnew, 2007: p.359).

This kind of struggle for recognition has remained the main hindrance for most of the African people even in this day and age where multiculturalism seems to be dominant in the Canadian society.

Emotional turmoil

After we thought we had jumped the hurdle of the housing issue, it was the constant sickness and visiting the doctor's office. It was even tougher when we visited our doctor on a cold day while traveling by bus with four kids. At the time, we did not have a car of our own. The children would all be crumped together to get some warmth from each other. On the bus, people would look at us, some with sympathy, and others strangely because of the way children were shivering and not well dressed for the weather.

Emotions of self-pity would fill my mind, thinking back of how I used to be driven around in my own cars. Sometimes I would console myself with feelings that one day this public transportation would end and my children would eventually be driven in their family car. Those who have gone through this experience may have a sense of what I am talking about. It was a very testing moment for me personally. I recalled the good times when I was a "woman of status", a wife of a dignitary who was always driven around any time she wanted. I was in a new environment with four little kids, faced with the challenge of cold weather. I could not explain to these kids how dad and mum used to have a good life with our own cars and were always driven around whenever we wanted. I was not sure whether it was necessary for them to know all about our past. Besides, even if I were to talk to them, they would not understand.

Weather dressing

Coming to this new society, I had no knowledge about the weather, nor did I know how to dress my little boys with winter clothes, although it was already past winter and now spring time. I recall one afternoon going out for shopping with two of my youngest kids dressed in pajamas and my third born was freezing to death! When we arrived home, the boy was very sick because, I had no knowledge how to dress kids with warm clothes in spring. The strange thing is dressing the kid with pajamas and then going to the market not concerned of what people thought! I do not know what people perceived when they saw a woman carrying a baby on her back, and another being pulled along as we walked on the streets. This was the only way I knew how to dress a child in winter weather.

The power of community connections

Before the dreams could be revived, I felt I had to first change the way I spoke English in order to be accepted by people I socialized with. This was not a prerequisite for me to change my accent, but only to try to blend in because of people asking me repeatedly, "What did you say?" It appeared to be the best way to follow and indeed, it felt like it was going to work. I was motivated to take some baby steps of taking English courses where I could be taught how to change my accent. This was a dream come true because I was now going to be through with the huddle of people asking "What did you say?" Hearing that there was a school that could change the way I talked was the best option for me. As I started school, I found a different story than what I had anticipated. I was asked to take a General Education Diploma (GED)!

This was an opportunity for me where I was able to open up and talk about my frustrations about the lack of community connection. I talked about what I did in Uganda before going into exile. The instructors/teachers got interested in hearing my stories, and encouraged me to join social work. I was not familiar with the type of social work they had demonstrated to me. Theoretically, I knew it was working with people and listening to their stories or giving them a hand whenever they were in problems. I had no knowledge about community resources or schools that I could apply to. The teachers believed in me as I shared my personal life story while preparing me for the GED, which I passed. I also felt that there were people who finally believed in me.

The teachers were very determined to look for the applications and fill them out for me to get into a school where I could train as a social worker. They only brought them for me to sign. This was indeed an aspect of cross-cultural therapy. What I really needed was someone to guide me to go through the right path, which these teachers demonstrated. As many researchers of trauma survivors have identified, it is important that those counselors working with survivors of war be supportive and nonjudgmental toward trauma survivors, and "meet them where they are" regardless of how long ago the trauma occurred or how severe it was (Bryant & Harvey, 2000). The instructors put themselves in my shoes. They came out of their comfort zones to help an immigrant woman who needed guidance and direction.

Before getting accepted into the program, I had to be interviewed. This was my first Canadian interview. As I had gotten used to telling my life story of war, the instructor who interviewed me heard bits of it in that one-hour interview time. When I finished the oral part, I could not believe how friendly the person was. I was waiting for such a tough interview where I was expected to speak some English that did not have an accent. I had been used to being asked, "What kind of accent is this?" What I heard from this instructor was about his cultural heritage, which was similar to mine. Creese (2006) points out:

> Thus language creates a double disjunction in African women's lived experience in Vancouver: first, as women who hail from Commonwealth nations, English is understood as one of their own languages and, taking their own fluency for granted, the erasure of English competency is troubling and surprising; and second, the dominant discourse of Canada as a pluralist multicultural society makes perplexing the everyday denigration of the 'foreign', be it accents, educational credentials, or people (p.17).

The person who conducted the interview was of First Nations descent. He shared a little bit about his First Nations' history and what colonialists did to his people after sharing my own personal experience about the infamous "Idi Amin." He understood where I came from. This instructor made my life very easy and comfortable in this interview. He also knew the aspect of cross cultural counseling and cultural competence which is very relevant in most of my work today with mental health people and my fellow African immigrant and refugee women.

I believe this instructor had three distinguished attitudes that are always vital in dealing with cultures that are not your own, especially when dealing with people that have had traumatic past experiences: universalism, cultural uniqueness, and the rejection of one's own culture of origin. After doing my oral interview, I knew I had passed and was heading for a future that would finally rekindle my dreams. Three weeks later I was accepted into Langara's Social Services Program to start a career that has led me to help families with relatives suffering with mental illness and also with other immigrant women that have had similar experience as mine. It was also the beginning of getting out of isolation. I believe the confidence in me came as a result of getting people who cared and understood my circumstances without holding me accountable by the way I spoke English. To this day I still recall those instructors who put themselves in my shoes.

This instructor acted out of professionalism, but his approach in talking to me has made me reach where I am, where I could have given up on the first appearance before an interview panel in the Canadian society, especially when I had a vivid negative "passport" which I always carried around as I talked to people, "my accent"!

I went into school for my social services certificate program even though I had vowed not to associate myself with any African people, or work with an organization that works with them whatsoever. I do not know where this anger came from. Sometimes when there are unresolved traumatic issues, this is what happens to people! Shortly after earning my certificate, I found myself working with women who came wounded as I was. Some talked about being raped in the presence of their husbands. Others related their traumatic experiences to being ostracized by their community after being raped. Such stories were common occurrences in our talks. Hearing their stories was even more traumatic than mine.

I was not yet sure what I wanted to do professionally because I still faced the lack of a support network. What I wanted was to focus on my studies and fulfill my dreams of "a woman of status". I did not know by what means I would achieve this dream. The "woman of status" mentality did not appear to be a big issue to focus on, but something that I had always wanted to be. However, my going to school was not without challenges.

I was embarrassed by my own accent. Each time I was in class, I feared to be asked, "What did you say?" Thankfully, this never became a problem for my instructors. Most of them encouraged me by telling me how much they loved to hear me speak "my accent." Their encouragement was genuine. I could even tell by the way they motivated me to pursue further studies in order to help other African immigrant women. These instructors rekindled the vision that I had, "helping poor women" who needed a listening ear!

Even though I went to this social service program, I was not sure what I was going to do after finishing my first step of education in

Canada. But I still had my vision, of being a "woman of status" which I was sure no one could take from me. Joyce Meyer points out:

> Vision allows us to look past our circumstances and see our God-given potential. Mother Teresa traveled to India with only 2 pennies, but she had a vision…and eventually became a modern day hero whose life forever changed the way we view the poor and needy. Vision will help you to look beyond where you are right now and open the door for God to do the impossible through your life (p.5).

Without vision, people perish; people make decisions that collapse before they reach their destiny because of lack of vision. In my case, I believe it was the initial dream that I came with as I migrated to Canada that inspired me during those times when women shared their own experiences with me. I was able to continue with my goal of going the extra mile by going back to school in order to inspire others who might have gone through the same experience as mine. I cannot say that I am over the experience of being asked about my accent and the consciousness that comes along with talking to people who are not from my ethnic group, mindful that the "what did you say" is going to come up after finishing my sentence.

Gladly, the more time I have spent working with people from all walks of life, the more comfortable I have become. I no longer get bothered by the questioning of "what accent is this and where about is this accent from"? I have had clients, family members and professionals alike who have told me about my accent, but this is not an issue that bothers me whatsoever anymore. This is due to the confidence that I have gained doing my job. What I have focused on is remembering that it is not the accent that does the job, but the ability to carry out my work; to serve the people that need my support. The courage to do my professional job in Canada did not come about without the support of those who believed in me. Where I met resistance due to my accent, my colleagues stepped in to support me. To this day, I still cherish their support and friendship, especially at times when I wanted to simply quit working in the Canadian society.

One woman demonstrates her frustration as she started looking for a job in the Canadian institutions:

...And one particular experience I had to confront was fitting in with my accent and wouldn't be able to get a job. And one friend a teacher called me to her school to do storytelling and that same friend told me that the children wouldn't understand my accent. I went to the same school all the same and did my story telling, and the children not only understood my accent, they wanted my stories. So that experience of the accent... it was new to me, because where I come from we have about three hundred languages (Comfort, focus group, 2004).

After my ordeals in exile life, I had developed a different perspective in serving women. I cannot compare myself with heroines like Mother Teresa or Oprah Winfrey. Mine was just a simple vision and determination that anything is possible if you focus on it with encouragement from people around you or with a passion that you put on the vision. After finishing my certificate, it was not clear to me whether I wanted to pursue the goal of working with African women or not. I had started developing some fear about working with this group due to the trouble I experienced back in Africa. Everyone that looked Ugandan specifically was a reminder of my past trauma in that country. Besides, I had some suspicious feelings they were spies.

Working with this population was not something desirable for me. I still had to face the reality of schooling in Canada before I thought of other things, such as working with the African refugee and immigrant women. There was research that I needed to do, especially on a community or population that I was familiar with, which required that I go and look for information that related to African immigrant women in Vancouver, British Columbia.

I had to do what I was required by my school before I could begin planning for future work. To my disappointment, I searched all libraries and organizations, but could not find anything that had been documented about African immigrants and refugees in the Lower Mainland. I remember being told by my instructors to go to MOSAIC to look for any publications that would give me some information about this population, but found none. It was very frustrating for me specifically because I did not have much experience about other ethnic groups. I was still new, only two years in the country! The only group I felt would be of help to me to do research and produce good results was the African community. There was nothing that had been documented regarding

African immigrant women. This was the time I decided that something must be done about the African women. I knew there were so many stories that had never been told by these women and that they needed to be told.

At MOSAIC, I got connected to a woman who had just come to the country who was also looking for information regarding African women. We both tried to do something for this group of immigrants. I became one of the people that she got interested in working with, after we had met and shared some of our concerns and frustrations about the African community. Before I knew it, I got a call from someone who introduced herself as an executive director of an organization that serves immigrant groups.

She wanted me to go for a job interview to work with African immigrant women. I did not know who the person was; neither had I ever expressed any interest to work with African women. This I felt was nothing, but an act of God. We agreed on a time to meet for an interview. I told my instructor, who advised me not to allow anybody to use me for volunteer purposes. This was going to be my second interview in the country. The woman who called me happened to be a professor at the UBC School of Social Work who was also running an NGO in East Vancouver. She interviewed me and hired me on the spot.

The job was to work with African mothers who were living in isolation. I had also noticed from my own experience of isolation that at least a support group for African women needed to be started where they could meet and talk about their own frustrations in their new home. Such a request was taken seriously by MOSAIC in East Vancouver. The woman they connected me to, was of the same opinion due to her own frustrations of not getting AIR women to participate in her meetings. She was approached by this professor to start a program for the African women, which she declined. Instead she suggested my name, thus the Executive Director called me for an interview. Starting a new program for this population was not an easy adventure in a new society. The challenge was that working with the African community needed a lot of concentration and efforts.

People were scattered and it was not easy to motivate them to come for programs, partly because of their own fears of the political situations they were escaping from, thus lacking trust of the new system. However, even though working with these African women was challenging, it was an opportunity for me to learn about the similarities of the experiences that we all shared in our journey of pre-post-migration. I learnt that these women needed to be given a listening ear without judging them whatsoever. They needed a second chance in life after having gone through the horrors of wars and the sufferings they had in refugee camps. The backgrounds of these AIR women are very relevant to an understanding of their position in the host society. One woman explains and cries about her experience:

> ...our mental is not good and we think about our lives, our future in this country. We think about our kids, how we can look after our kids, keeping in mind that we have diplomas we can't use. We need to pay house rent, we need to pay bills, and we need to pay everything. That is why the Canadian government needs to change their system of dealing with us when we come to Canada. If you come here with your diploma, like now my diploma is sitting in my house (Yei: focus group # 1, 2007).

For these women, the post-immigration traumas are the challenges they came to present to me as I listened to their stories including: unemployment, discrimination, and cultural conventions, which enforce "keeping a low profile," economic victimization, and circumscribed personal mobility. The stories from the African women that I started working with in 1996 mirrored the changing nature of gender roles and expectations that have historically characterized the social organization of this particular community. Social relations and societal values have unquestionably been more confining to these African women, affording them little mobility compared to other ethnic immigrant women.

Breaking this cultural mold, African women come with high expectations, but are only shattered by lack of understanding by the system they have passed through before they make it to their final destination. While the policies have been changed, organizations have developed best practices; the stories from people who receive services are still the same. Their stories, too, demonstrate how African women are craving a space for themselves in the social landscape of their receiving societies. They offer insight into the changing perceptions of the long lasting and widely held image of passive, voiceless, docile and dependent women who can only be viewed "as tails" rather than as independent actors.

African immigrant and refugee women come and travel journeys that are full of sadness and trauma, and yet have thrived only by the grace and mercy of God. When you listen to our stories, you will understand that our journeys have not been rosy as some employers, counselors or co-workers may imagine. It is obvious that one cannot compare a woman coming from a refugee camp no matter how many Degrees they came with, to perform or present themselves as a freshman from the University of British Columbia, University of Victoria or Toronto. As Jon Allen, a psychologist at the Menninger Clinic in Topeka, Kansas and author of *Coping with Trauma: A Guide to Self-Understanding* (1995), reminds us, there are two components to a traumatic experience: the objective and the subjective.

> It is the subjective experience of the objective events that constitutes the trauma... The more you believe you are endangered, the more traumatized you will be... Psychologically, the bottom line of trauma is overwhelming emotion and a feeling of utter helplessness. There may or may not be bodily injury, but psychological trauma is coupled with physiological upheaval that plays a leading role in the long-range effects (p.14).

Other scholars have demonstrated how trauma does not only affect the emotional and psychological aspects, but the entire body system. Perry (1997) explains, to some degree all of the organ systems in the human body have "memory." This ability to carry elements of previous experience forward in time is the basis of the immune, the neuromuscular and neuroendocrine systems. Through complex physiological processes, elements of experience can even be carried across generations even after the healing has occurred. There will always be some memories of some sort. Such elements of the collective experience of what happened in the past, be it rape, witnessing of killings and political displacements, such memories can be carried on for generations even if healing had already happened, as one participant puts it:

> We used to wake up with pain all over the body. There were snakes in our houses. I am talking but before you live in a camp you cannot understand. I was young seeing my parents suffering. Feeding on the same food every day. My father had to go and hunt birds so we could change the diet or at least eat something

different because each day it was the same diet. Cooking on smoky wired wood every day caused my mother to die with cancer. Every time I talk about these problems in the camp, I cry. Due to camp problems, my brother escaped to a different camp in Zimbabwe hoping to find a better life, but life did not change, it was the same as where he left us. He was infected by cholera, which finally killed him. Life in the refugee camp was so hard. One cannot say life in the camp is good. Even now I am here still sorrowful in my heart up to this present day. (Monna: Focus group # 1: Dec. 2007).

African immigrant and refugee women come wounded and exhausted from the baggage that we have carried as a result of the political upheavals. Many are affected by displacement due to natural or manmade calamities, however, women travel from their countries of origin long journeys of trauma after trauma before they finally make it to Canada. Only a few of us come with sane minds. We are wounded by the rapes and starvation in refugee camps.

There is also the loss of social status after having endured hardships during our long journeys and the abandonment of not knowing where our husbands or children would be. These are some of the issues we come carrying as we enter our new home countries. Subsequently, it becomes very difficult for these women to maintain their sanity when part of them, their very precious friends or children are suffering in refugee camps or even in prison. It is obvious that we are faced with a lot of shame and guilt as a result of these mishaps.

In most cases what we need is not only psychological platitudes and to simply be listened to, but to be encouraged and to be informed on what to do to survive in the new environment. I believe many other women who have had their own challenges, would agree with me. It is a sympathetic attitude towards trauma survivors and a listening ear that would sooth the traumatic experiences that women experienced. What they need is someone who would say "I know where you are coming from, I understand that your journey has not been that easy, come along with me and I will show you doors of opportunities." It does not help to get guidance from someone who will judge you by the way you speak English. It is important for these women to be accepted and to feel that they belong. If they feel rejected, this becomes a reminder that the journey is not yet over. Quoting one woman from Vijay Agnew (2007), interview by Creese, she points out:

> To belong to Canada is to be treated equally; I think that's when I would think I belong here. Right now, they look at me and right away they think that I don't belong here, you know. So belonging is to be seen as if I equally belong here, not you know as somebody who is passing through (p.352).

In conducting interviews and focus groups for this book, it was very overwhelming to hear each woman's account, but at the same time seeing the pride that these women brought with them no matter the brokenness that they all carried. They gave me joy as I saw the hope in them. Being the person on the other side of the table, as a counselor and motivator, I realized that these women needed people who understood the genesis of their long journey. Remember, I had vowed not to work with this group during my school time because of my own fears from past experiences. Strange as it may sound, the very thing I feared is exactly what I happen to enjoy and has become the driving force of writing this book.

The African community is a group of people that I have worked with over the years and have found solace to my own fears. I have found relief and comfort as I work with each woman with their unique experiences. Even after I had had the fears, but I finally connected with people who shared similar experiences as mine. We all worked journeys of hardships; lack of trust, but eventually found that we are friends due to our pains of past traumatic experiences. I saw that I was not alone in my own struggles, fears, shame and social disconnections. I found women who had similar experiences of isolation as I listened to their untold stories of resilience and triumph.

During my first years of work with this group, I slowly found healing from my own frustrations of post-traumatic experiences as I listened to these women's stories. Stanley (Nov. 2007), in his monthly *In Touch Magazine* argues:

Yet nature itself proves the strange and paradoxical reality that healing really can come from the most unlikely of sources. Ironically if we are to be bitten by a rattlesnake, the serum that would save your life would be derived from rattlesnake venom itself (ps.28-29).

Indeed, the very people that I had resented working with were the very ones with whom I found strength and help. When we are faced with our own baggage, it is very difficult to think of other people carrying similar baggage. Listening to these women's life experiences was very therapeutic for me personally. I heard women's stories of rape, starvation and overstaying in refugee camps. Some of them shared stories of how they slept on the roadside on empty stomachs. There were those who had spent fifteen years in refugee camps and appeared as if they were from a war zone. Some of them shared their strengths and how they pulled through day-by-day, not wanting to let their families know what was pressing them hard on their hearts, especially in situations where the husbands had become helpless and not being the family providers.

I heard stories of how some women put on happy faces to ensure that the family did not feel demoralized, exactly like what I felt when I was going through my own ordeals in Congo and here in Canada. As I worked with these women, and listened to their interesting yet very painful stories, I realized that women are very resilient in all aspects. They only need someone to give them the motivation and guidance on how to do things, because I saw in them aspects of big dreams, whose joy and aspirations were never in vein. One friend sent me the following note:

> One flaw in women, women have strengths that amaze men. They bear hardships and they carry burdens, but they hold happiness, love and joy. They smile when they want to scream. They sing when they want to cry. They cry when they are happy and laugh when they are nervous. They fight for what they believe in. They stand up to injustice. They don't take 'no' for an answer when they believe there is a better solution. They go without so their family can have. They go to the doctor with a frightened friend. They love unconditionally. They cry when their children excel and cheer when their friends get awards. They are happy when they hear about a birth or a wedding. Their hearts break when a friend dies. They grieve at the loss of a family member, yet they are strong when they think there is no strength left... However, if there is one flaw in women, it is that they forget their worth (Friend: Oct 22, 2007).

Every woman whose story I have listened to has had some aspects of what the above quotation explains. As I worked with them in my first years as a professional in my new country, Canada, there were also some emotional traumas that were rekindled. Women shared horrific accounts of abuse and trauma in the countries they were fleeing from. I was informed of the difficulties they faced in their integration process into the Canadian society. There were times when we all cried together as we shared our own stories. Another woman recounts her frustrations during her integration process:

> Every day we sleep we are sick crying and crying thinking about this. We will die in Canada, slowly. They see you walking on the street we are sick, we don't have to be sick because we think a lot and we don't have to be sick. Sometime the girl is walking on the street; they want to jump out in the blue. You see most of the accidents occur on the streets, in the intersection because you are walking thinking what to eat the next day (Yei: Focus group # 1, 2007).

This is what I had missed in my first years in Canada. I needed someone who would sit down with me and talk about life's experiences. For these women, integrating successfully into Canadian society was very difficult because they could not find good jobs that utilized their prior training and education, the institutional racist policies compounded with the unacceptance of the host society and its reaction towards them became barriers for their integration. Another woman argues:

> We need help; we need people to really guide us because we don't have any access to go forward into the market world. You people who are really well connected should help us and make us know that this is the way we have to go through. Let them help us so that people may get more zeal to help us work in facilities (Kabira: focus group, Dec.2007).

Many of the women recounted that lack of these essentials escalated their stress level, which is associated with depression and various mental health problems (Beiser, 1999). I also shared my own experience of isolation, which took a huge toll on my emotional and physical health. When these women heard my own stories and saw what I was doing, some became amazed to see that there is hope even after hardships. I was consistently asked about how I was able to go to school all the while carrying such a load of trauma that I had not shared with anybody. Our sharing of past and present experiences was therapeutic in many aspects.

We all came out of the session knowing that other women need to be informed, that isolation is not the solace for pre-post migration traumas, but rather sharing stories is the only healing approach to our experiences.

The twisting road to high education

After realizing that my social work certificate was not enough to enable me to work with this hurting population, I had to pursue further education while working part-time with this group. Juggling school and work was not an easy thing to do as a mother, housewife and worker. It is only because of the support from my family, my supervisors at work, and even the women I worked with, that I was able to get my diploma in the same field. Although I had the support of this network, the guilt of not attending to my house responsibilities, especially my children and husband was too enormous. I decided to take evening courses, although I will not inform you that this helped with the guilt either. That meant going a whole day from 8 am to 9 pm away from my family!

It was such a sacrifice to take this adventure. There were times when I could not concentrate in class because my children were home alone. This created some psychological and emotional tension. I knew they were home alone because my husband worked evening shifts. I still feared if the protection officer came to our house, would take our children away. I had lost trust in the system because, if anything happened we could lose our children since our family file was still open due to an earlier case. I only managed going to school because my husband went to work after he had brought the children from school and prepared dinner. Although it was a workable arrangement, my prior experience with the Ministry of Children and Family Development (MCFD) could not make me feel at ease.

My own experience with the system was similar to those of AIR families especially when they wanted to upgrade their academic requirements. According to Creese (2006) and Agnew in her interviews with African women, this is how some women describe their personal experiences:

Kalumbi: Africans, we depend on extended family back home and without an extended family you feel like your child is not going to grow up as a community person. Back in Africa the extended family take care of your children if you are [at] work, so you may not even employ anybody. They help you in shaping their morals. And when we got here it even becomes so difficult even to invite one of the relatives. Because here a relative is not considered as a family member, unless she is your mother, or your wife or your parents. But your brother is not considered as a family, which is very bad to Africans, because in Africa a brother is a family member, very serious family member. A sister is... my son would be calling my brother his father. My sister, he would be calling him his aunt, seriously so, and my wife's sister would be his mother. But in Canadian life, that is not acceptable and it is very hurting to immigrants. And most families here have broken down because of lack of that kind of connection. It can make the family very dysfunctional. (Interview # 32)

These explanations speak volumes of frustrations that many of the families go through as they try to settle while advancing their lives in Canada. It is evident from the above quotations that without extended family and neighbors responsible for each other's children, the full burden of domestic work and child rearing is placed on the parents' shoulders, which is very difficult for a new family that is trying to make ends meet. Most immigrants come from cultures where extended family is the norm. When you are an immigrant, there is a lot that you have to go through. First of all, there is no support network or extended family that one could depend on.

In my case, I constantly wanted to quit my program in order to be with my children because I felt uncomfortable in class, not knowing what was happening with my boys. How could I be a productive student when there was divided attention between school and family? My husband continuously encouraged me not to quit because this would not give the children a good impression. It was important that I finish so that I had something that I would use as an example to our boys. I was the role model to them.

Sometimes immigrant and refugee women need people who can support them to pursue their dreams. I found my husband such a huge support. Some of the few friends I met also encouraged me that it was the best thing for a mother to do for her children to emulate. They specifically told me this would help my boys to also have something to look forward to as they grow; no matter how painful the process might look. Osteen (2007) writes:

When you are tempted to get discouraged, don't you dare go find five other friends who are discouraged and sit around discussing your problems. Find somebody happy to cheer you up. Get around people who will inspire you to rise higher. Be careful with whom you associate, especially when you feel emotionally vulnerable, because negative people can steal the dream right out of your heart (p. 29).

Having these friends and husband around inspired me to continue with my dream. Hearing what they told me was motivational and I felt at peace for some time. I remember one friend specifically pointing out that what I was doing was a positive sacrifice that my children would cherish for life no matter how I may look at it. She told me that it would work as a model that would support and inspire them to pursue their own carriers. Osteen (2007) continues:

Surround yourself with people who encourage you, people who will build you up... Don't surround yourself with a bunch of "yes-men." On the other hand, don't tolerate a bunch of negative, critical, "can't do it" people who are close to you... but people who plan to do something significant with their lives... You may come from a family of defeat, failure, and negativism, but this is your time to rise above that morass. Start stretching your faith once again. Get up each morning expecting good things to happen. Don't settle for mediocrity; never let good enough be good enough. You too will discover that the dream is true!! (p.31)

I am ever grateful for all the inspirations that I received from a friend like that, and then my husband for allowing me to continue with my academic career. Yes, it is important that we surround ourselves with people that will encourage us and walk us the path that is meaningful, especially when we are on the verge of giving up on our dreams. Every one of my children supported me in a way. I recall moments when I came home tired and with such headaches, these little boys would put their little hands on my head and shoulder; and start praying for me. It was sure a soothing moment as I heard their sweet voices saying, "God give mum strength as she goes on with school, and please God, take away mum's headache." Oh, you should have been there to see these little boys say a prayer of encouragement to their mother! What more could I have wanted from these innocent kids who knew nothing that was going on in my life, but only to offer a prayer that I mostly needed when I was totally exhausted from both work and school!

Like many women who go to school at a mature age, I was in class one evening and had the need to call home and find out how my boys were doing, only to find no response in the house. I tried twice but there was no response. My heart started racing. "What has gone on with my children?" were the questions that I started racing with. I quickly had to go and explain my situation to my professor who later allowed me to go home. To arrive home there were no children in the house. My worst fear was that the MCFD workers again came to my house and took the most precious thing I have in life - my children! Do we immigrants have to fear professionals? That is what happens up to this day! This is the nightmare most immigrants face.

As noted by Wasik (2006) in her interviews with African immigrant women, and their experiences of parenting which were equally as traumatizing as finding someone to entrust their children. Here is what one woman explained:

> You have to work, but you can't find work because you have a small child. Where [do] I suppose to leave her? How am I supposed to find work? If my husband works, just by himself, the money isn't enough. And I want to put money away for my daughter's education, for when she grows up. So, I also have to work. But where can I leave her? The daycares are too expensive: eight hundred dollars. Yeah, eight hundred dollars each month at the daycare. And so if you are earning eight dollars an hour, and the daycare is eight hundred-then you have your rent. So, if you pay for daycare, you wouldn't have money for rent...but I need to work. If I don't work, I won't survive here. And if I don't work, I am always stuck at home and I won't have any money, and I won't have money for daycare, to even have the money to work (Interview #16).

This story is an situation that most of the women go through as they try to reconstruct their lives in a new society. In my case I do not know how I managed to survive these daily difficulties of leaving my children at the risk of knowing that anytime I might find them taken by the same system that I felt was to protect us using a holistic approach, so that we could reach the standards of two income earners. I depended on my first born who was 14 years-old then. I knew he was of legal age to keep his siblings. After thirty minutes of not knowing where I could get hold of them, I started calling everyone that I knew to find out where my boys could have gone. Unfortunately nobody knew exactly what had gone on with these boys.

After a long ordeal of about forty minutes, my boys arrived at home around 8 pm. When I saw them, I simply called out, "where did you go boys?" There was no need why I would even get angry at them. I was solely to blame for leaving these boys at home. I felt it was my responsibility as a mother to stay at home and look after my children. I believe this was a myth. I forgot that I had to upgrade my education in order for the family to be able to cope with the living standards of a two income earning family.

After we had all settled down, my eldest son told me how he had soccer and did not want to leave his little brothers at home without anybody. He further explained how he asked the person that gave him a ride to soccer if he could also take his little brothers because he had no one to leave them with. What a brilliant idea this young man had! I do not call this experience unique, but reflective of so many families that try to cope with the economic hardships that they encounter, especially when the Income Assistance is not enough to support a family of more than four people. Most of the African families are not as small as those in the Western World. Besides, when we come with these large families, it is not easy to afford a daycare subsidy as some women have explained in this narrative. It becomes even a dilemma when you want to be a good parent, stay home and be there when children come from school. Besides, you want to support the family economically. Another woman whose frustrations were like mine points out:

> Parenting is a challenge. You cannot afford a baby sitter and yet you want to work. You want to go to school you can't pay daycare fees. No extended family to help with childcare rearing. It is each person with his or her own problems. When you cannot work or leave children you end up on a cycle of social welfare, which has its own limitations (Wasik, 2006. p.18).

When faced with such parenting challenges, it becomes problematic for parents to be able to discipline their children. In my case, thankfully with all these experiences, I finished my diploma, but was faced with a challenge of getting a decent job that would allow me support my husband.

Despite the lack of adequate employment, I felt rewarded working and sharing my personal experience with women as I integrated in the new society. I was able to give these women what I acquired in a different way than I had anticipated. My perception of sharing personal experiences of life pre-post-migration became the motivation under which I developed passion to work with this group of immigrant women. Sharing about my struggle with loneliness and the painful experience that came with it, which affected everything about my well-being was used as a reward for other women to get strength to face the challenges of a new society.

Juggling with school, parenting and work became the base of my aspiration to pursue other dreams than the ones I had anticipated to follow - working with mainstream organizations! It is apparent to me that my going to school to study social work was an adventure that would give me a different perceptive on the issues related to the effects of trauma resulting from pre-post migration. For reasons explained in the previous sections of this chapter, it is one of the baby steps that we each take that lead us to achieve our dreams. They may not be the exact dreams that we had hoped for; however, what is important is if the dreams are able to give hope to those who are hopeless. Sometimes you find yourself benefiting from it in a very different way. Through the women's narratives and my own experience, it is a common phenomenon that our stories are not only of courage, but also of aspirations that we come with, to try and build ourselves as we settle in our new home country, Canada.

I did not expect to find unfriendly environment of professionals. I expected to find people who were friendly and welcoming. I was shocked at the welcome I received, especially by the manager. I had questions rather than answers to my fears of what we were told before we left Congo for Canada. We were told Canada is a multicultural and inclusive society. This gave us peace of mind, knowing that we would find a welcoming society. Besides, United Nations High Commission for Refugees offices in Third World Countries portrays Canada's reputation for human rights as excellent and this portrayal of the West gives false hope of what refugees expect as they arrive in Canada.

In Wasik's (2006) interviews with African Service providers, she is informed of inflated expectations that women are not given an accurate description of what life would be like when they arrive in Canada. Service providers contend that African refugees do not understand the extent to which the Canadian system is a classified society, and the daily pattern of struggles the working poor and unemployed suffer as they integrate.

In her study, many of the service providers shared their own experiences working with this population and some of the stories they hear from the women. The following is a descriptive of what was highlighted in her findings:

> In coming to this country, they think they're coming to a place where there's no suffering... but when they come here, they thought they were in a friendly environment. It takes them by surprise... It's like, you're looking at something pretty and beautiful, and yet, when you reach for it, it's not there. You know, that does something to your psyche. (Int. # 1: pg. 12)

Another woman explains her traumatic experience as a result of the system that was hostile towards her:

> I think that one of the biggest traumas is for women who leave their country with a different vision of the new country they are going to. Because mostly, when we hear about the West, when we hear about Canada, we think of happiness, we think peace, we think love, we think unity. So when you are in Africa, you want to come to this place, you want to come and experience this difference, this new life... And then we come here, we realize that no, there's no Garden of Eden. It's only there for some people, not everyone... So you come here and you hope you are going to enjoy the goodness, but you realize there is no goodness, that it's a struggle. And life becomes a struggle that is forever a struggle. (Int. # 20: pg. 20)

Service providers are constantly faced with situations that are overwhelming as they listen to accounts of traumatic stories from women, it is evidenced from their narratives that life for these women is still as traumatic as it was before coming to Canada. Consequently, service providers including myself and many others who have had direct contact with women from Sub-Saharan Africa feel that the new traumas of this population have to be understood in the context of the previous suffering.

Additionally, their expectations for a better life upon arrival in their new society have to be taken into consideration. Unfortunately at that time, the experience of this author suggests that employment equity measures generate such a huge discrepancy and backlash that many of us immigrant women suffer in our work places no matter how much one may want to appease their employers. What matters is if the chemistry between the two individuals does not connect, it cannot work. To me, I felt if you are an immigrant woman, you can only perform well if your accent is local. I questioned whether it is the accent that performs the task that one is given or the ability one has to do the job. Osteen (2007) points out about his own experience when someone believed in him, someone who encouraged him, without criticizing him despite his size and height. He says:

> It's amazing what we can accomplish when we know that somebody really believes in us...that coach took a little time to make a big difference. He took time to instill confidence in me. If we're going to bring out the best in people, we too need to sow seeds of encouragement (p.135).

This statement speaks volumes to us who have had our share of frustrations. If immigrants are being brought here after having had some ugly experiences, they need people to invest in them seeds of hope, not to shatter their dreams criticizing the way they look or speak.

It is obvious these women have some trauma of one aspect or another. The employers have to be informed they are dealing with people who are carrying baggage that they have never shared with anybody. Even if they had, they still have scars that linger around them, that need only a listening ear for the healing to occur. Herman J. (1997) explains: "The reconstruction of trauma is never entirely completed; new conflicts and challenges at each new stage of the lifecycle will inevitably reawaken the trauma and bring some new aspect of the experience to light" (p.195).

Re-traumatization by daily life

In other words, these people experience re-traumatization every moment they are ostracized by the very people who they felt would give a helping hand! What the receiving countries have to understand is that some of the AIR women are angry at what happened to them pre-migration. They were uprooted from their familiar surroundings due to political motives by a few individuals. It will take these women a long time before they finally get through with their emotions if they can't find a welcoming environment that gives them hope.

Unfortunately, my accent not being accepted in the workplace has been a common phenomenon for many immigrants. I questioned why sociologists and other academics in the field of migration studies were not paying attention to the complex issues involved in the perceptions of language fluency or processes by which racialization mediates embodied boundaries of immigration. English accent is one such identifier. It identifies the speaker as either local or extra local, hence Canadian or immigrant (Creese & Kambere, 2003). Thus, language is lived as a significant problem for those who speak English with "an accent." Storrie (1987) also explains the implications of being labeled:

> Immigrant women with an accent...the term immigrant women itself is problematic because it indicates racist and class bias in the treatment of certain groups of women. The term implies and presupposes a legal relation, in the everyday world, only women of color, notably from Third World countries, who do not speak English or who speak English with an accent (other than British or American), are seen to be as immigrant women (p.142-3).

This contention supports what we African women have identified in every aspect of social interaction as barriers posed by our African accent: the accent acts 1) as a barrier to full or equitable participation in particular institutions, particularly in the labor market, and 2) as a more general barrier to acceptance or belonging (Creese and Kambere, 2003). In one of the focus groups that I conducted early on (Kambere, 2004), one woman whom I will call Onelia asserts her frustration about the questioning of her African accent: "Sometime when I am at work someone asks me, 'excuse me, where does that accent come from? And I am like... "Do you have some problems with my accent?"

Many of us who speak with specific accents find this questioning and experience very demeaning, especially when it has nothing to do with your job. Questioning my ability to conduct my work effectively due to my accent became a common phenomenon. I recall one day in this department I referred to earlier, being called in the office to meet with the regional supervisor to discuss my performance. The team manager started by explaining my work habits and what she felt was necessary for the supervisor to know. At this point they had called for me a union Shop Steward, something I had never experienced! I had no understanding about a Shop Steward. The manager then said, "Maybe it is because of her English that is why she is not performing according to standards." Wow! It is the English language that performs the work, not the ability that one carries to the job!

The supervisor together with my Shop Steward had nothing to say at that point. They simply kept quiet because I believe they had their own concerns about what my accent had to do with my work performance. Unfortunately to this manager, I feel to this day, used my accent to justify her view that I had an inability to perform as she expected. There was no offensive word that I had said to anybody, but a matter of our chemistry not connecting. I was so disappointed to the point that I felt I should dig a hole in the ground and simply disappear.

First of all, this is not what I expected to hear. I am a woman with my African accent, and then my boss telling me, it is because of her "English" was very condescending. I was numb and stunned at her comments. Was she waiting to tell me this in front of these two individuals? Unfortunately, the accent problem continues to be a barrier and an issue that not only did I face with my manager, but other women I have worked with shared similar experiences. Like one woman comments: (Mapendo, focus group by Creese and Kambere, 2003, p.12) "It seems that somehow they put you in a spot where you become defensive. You have to defend how you talk."

Another woman in the same focus group points out her affirmation about her stand in regards to government sector jobs:

> I feel the same way as you all do about accents. After finishing my university degree, I feel I don't want to go and work in institutions where people will not listen to what I say, but only to correct my accent, which I have no control of (ibid).

It is sad in all these incidents that living in a multicultural society that is supposed to accept all people despite their sex, skin color, and religious background, and yet we still see people being judged by the very people who should be guiding and supporting them. Most of these participants come to Canada after having gone through a lot of trauma and yet the very people who should be helping them to resettle are exacerbating their trauma.

My experience with my employer became a rubber stamp that remained in my mind for some time. The questions that tormented me most were: How can someone criticize me about my English when it is an obvious "passport" that I carry with me everywhere I go? It was very difficult to understand whether this person knew that I was an African, whose accent could not be separated from the individual "me." I felt this manager just wanted the message to arrive and that is what she was waiting to tell me. It really affected me such that even in my other interactions, it was very difficult to freely interact well or communicate without being conscious that I was going to be judged by the way I speak English. I felt alone as I sat in her office with these two other guests who were as speechless as I was.

What could I have done after someone telling me that my English was the cause of my inability to perform or carry out some tasks? Again, it was like telling a physically disabled person and spelling it out in their face that this is how you look, and therefore, you look different. It was a moment that I regretted having worked with people who judged me by my accent. All these months I had been working with this department, I realized why I was always ostracized while those who spoke the Canadian accent always congregated or were put in specific cluster that this manager had created.

I recall during that same period of being ostracized, a student had come to do her practicum at the same organization. She asked me as we were having a walk. Her comments were: "You are always isolated from your colleagues." I did not want to say anything to her because I was not confident sharing my own frustrations with someone whom I had just met. Besides, I was not sure whether the question was genuine or an undercover investigation. I could not trust anybody who even came with a genuine reason. I believe this girl might have come with a sincere heart, but how could I have known after I had gone through the trauma of being criticized because of this "African accent"?

Some of the women in the African community have had similar experiences where their English language has worked against them. Quoting women's stories from Creese and Kambere (2003 focus group) about accent, as illustrated by the following statement:

I find this language as a tool that has been used against us and it is unfortunate that at this time we are still held accountable because of our accent. But if they could understand that, Canadian government which accepts immigrants, this language shouldn't be a barrier for people because it is dehumanizing. It is not that we don't know English. I think I know English. It is about Canadian or English accent. If the British cannot speak Nyangore as the way I speak it. I had an English lady in high school, she spoke my language fluently but when it came to accent it was different...So I think these people who are doing this research they should highlight the language barrier as a systemic barrier that was put within the system to put us down. I went to the university, I did all the papers, and you discriminate against me (Mabunda, focus group, 2003, p. 17).

It is apparent from the above explanations that people with the so called heavy accents are typically barred from employment. Moreover, when accent is being used as a tool to discriminate against these African women, one wonders how an African accent can be separated from an African body (Creese & Kambere, 2003). Another woman laments:

What I also found is, I made my resume and when they read it, it was excellent and then called me for the job interview. When I started to answer some of the questions they asked on the phone, "where are you from?" Then I said "from Africa." When did you land as an immigrant?" I said "in Africa we also are trained in English." "No wonder, your accent is too heavy, we cannot understand you (Nora, focus group, 2003, p.17).

The above women's accounts are not uncommon. They came with good qualifications, but were disqualified by the way they speak English! In my case, after I had been blatantly told about my English, I was confused and felt disillusioned, so isolated, and unwanted in this department. I had my Shop Steward around and when we finished the meeting, she said, "I do not think that you will survive in this office." It was obvious that I could not stand the stigma and the shame that came as a result.

First of all, during these meetings, there had been a lot of crying. It was even very difficult for me to focus on my work thereafter. Each colleague that I tried to talk with, I felt they knew what had happened. This is true because they saw how I was always summoned to go for meetings after the regional manager had started frequenting the office. It was even worse being the only black woman on the block/office! I could not survive no matter how strong I wanted to be. Indeed I felt lonely in this organization, and "Loneliness is one of man's most painful and feared emotions. Many people consider isolation, disconnectedness, and abandonment excruciating especially during periods of crisis" (Stanley 2010), p. 37). This was true with me in that organization. I could not perform to my ability, even the simplest task was hard for me to do.

I was faced with choices between continuous humiliations at working or quit this job and pursue my education and finish my Bachelor of Social Work (BSW). All the memories of my past trauma resurfaced. I thought I had healed from my ugly experiences, but here I was faced with rejection. Judith Herman (1997) explains:

Long after the danger is past, traumatized people relive the experience even as though it was continuously recurring in the present. They cannot resume the normal course of their lives, for the trauma repeatedly interrupts. It is as if time stops at the moment of trauma. The traumatic moment becomes encoded in an abnormal form of memory, which breaks spontaneously into consciousness, both as a flashback during waking states and as traumatic nightmares during sleep. Small, seemingly insignificant reminders can also evoke these memories, which often return with all the vividness and emotional force of the original event. Thus, even normally safe environments may come to feel dangerous, for the survivor can never be assured that she will not encounter some reminder of the trauma (p.37).

The rest of the time I was still in this office, I constantly suffered the torment of being judged because of my English accent. As a result, I developed a coping mechanism of simply becoming quiet. I never wanted to open my mouth out of fear that no one wanted to listen to me anyway. The comments stuck in my mind about my English such that I did not want to express my viewpoints in front of the team. I was faced with the challenge of whether I really wanted to continue to pursue my Social Work degree or change professions. I developed distaste for the social work profession with a passion.

I questioned whether this is how workers from other ethnic groups were treated in mainstream public sectors. The trauma escalated. I developed some physical problems, which I never wanted to share with my family. I feared for the worst. It was not even easy for me to visit my family doctor in fear of not wanting to narrate how the problem started. By narrating the situation, it would be a reminder of the mistreatment. Much as I developed physical problems, I heard of what other women such as Nora had gone through after their repeated trauma. She explains the physical toll of repeated rejection for jobs for which she was qualified and what this had contributed to her, a serious medical condition! She explains:

I developed medical problems because of rejection, not being accepted and not getting the jobs that I was qualified for. I developed medical problems and now I will not be able to work again. I have to take care of my medical problems (focus group; 2003 Creese & Kambere).

Another woman also recounts her experience while searching for employment: "The language is a barrier to integrate in the society because if you speak English in your accent, people will know that you are from Africa... and by the accent they cannot give you a job, or a house" (Kabugho, focus group 2003 Creese & Kambere). What else could a person like these women do after being judged affront because of their accent? These are all accounts of frustrations that African women encounter as they try to enter the Canadian job market. Other women's experience relates to my own experience as Wasik (2006) discovered from her own findings with the African women.

The problem of accents not only diminish refugee women's employment opportunities [one woman lamented] when she arrived for a job interview...but as one service provider commented, herself an African immigrant to Canada, you hear from someone that you can't speak, and you become shy. You hear it again, and you think twice. You say, 'okay, for me I can't talk again. I stay home. This is not my place. (Int. # 7).

Over several meetings with my Shop Steward, I shared my frustrations with her about how hard it had been for me to focus on my work. She finally realized that I had to choose between school and work. We both agreed that someone cannot be harassed or critically followed up like in my situation, and be a competent productive worker. After a long deliberation between work and school, I chose to quit work and continue with my school. I am pretty sure this is what my manager wanted to hear; to finally get rid of me! Besides, if I quit my job, that means no financial help from Employment Insurance, which indeed I did not receive because no one fired me; I chose to leave. This meant having no financial support for my school, but to simply depend on one income - my husband's. Nonetheless, the positive thing out of all this is, I was determined to pursue more education, which I did! It is an asset no one can ever take from me!

Quitting this job gave me an opportunity to do a full block practicum and study in order for me to finish my degree according to my prior plans. After several encounters, I came to accept that I needed to reflect on myself in order to function well in a society that continued to question my accent. I had to look at this situation in a more positive way, such that out of it I would learn how to handle other situations I might encounter. What I learnt through this experience was that when someone has power over you, that person has to exercise it with authority in order for the policy that governs the organization to be enforced. In one woman's account with the system, she identifies something strange that appeases me as I deal with people who come with different baggage.

> You know what? The strange thing is they don't realize that they are oppressing (us). I don't believe (they do). I could be wrong. Again, it's so systemic...they are acting the way they feel they should act. It's just part of them (Agnew, 2007: p.213).

Another woman laments: I think these managers are trained to intimidate employees (personal communication with a colleague, 2014). What I have also realized in North America, is the concept of individualism, which is very difficult for people who come from other cultures to appreciate, as an expression of power.

Agnew points out:

> In North America, a great deal of emphasis is placed on individualism and consequently, power is commonly viewed as an individual attribute...power is understood as the 'capacity

to get others to do one's will.' In situations where individual A enjoys higher status than individual B for example, in situations involving a supervisor and (social worker)...a teacher and a student, or a white and a black person, individual A has the capacity upheld by individual B. Since white people frequently enjoy higher social status, they can typically get black people or members of other racialized minority groups to conform to their will. When they are successful, white people may feel personally effective and good about themselves, while black or other racialized individuals may feel demeaned, 'like losers.'(Walker, 2002, quoted in Agnew 2007, p.213).

This quote resonates deeply with my own lived experience.

One might ask where I got the courage to walk around in public with all this baggage of shame. I had courage from my religious belief and the support from my faith sisters who continuously prayed with me. My dear reader, if you have walked this journey or if you are faced with situations that are pressing, such as rejection, you need to be assured that you are not alone! I was isolated and powerless in addition to my previous traumas that I was beginning to heal from. However, I can write these things with faith and courage that there is light at the end of the tunnel. Herman (1997) demonstrates:

> ...when the patient reclaims her own history and feels renewed hope and energy for engagement with life...telling a story has come to its conclusion, the traumatic experience truly belongs to the past. At this point, the survivor faces the tasks of rebuilding her life in the present and pursuing her aspirations for the future (p.195).

This story is my story.

Even after I was done with work, I was faced with the challenge of not finishing my school on time, as I had planned. My practicum supervisor arranged for another placement somewhere in the hospital. How could I even face this new person who would supervise me after I had gone through this previous placement? It was obvious that the next person would be informed of why the previous placement did not work. What a stigma! I went to this place with a lot of fear and embarrassment.

The fear to be judged or criticized again affects your very being to not even perform a simple task. I was affected by it in such a way that its impact affected both my physiological body and the chemical balance of my brain. I constantly felt dizzy. I never wanted to do anything or even go to work, but simply sleep. I was extremely stressed to the point that I was physically tired in a number of ways. In many cases when I was in the office, I would find myself sleeping at my desk.

To show you that fear is awful, every time my practicum supervisor called me into her office, I thought something was again wrong with my performance; I was always thinking of the past experience. Fear is an insidious weapon that attacks a person's very existence. It will keep you from making positive changes in your life, and thus retard your recovery from depression or past traumas. Herman (1997) points out:

> While a few resourceful individuals may be particularly resistant to the malignant psychological effects of [fear and] trauma, individuals at the other end of the spectrum may be particularly vulnerable (p.60).

I was vulnerable for any criticisms and I would take it as though I was the problem of my own making. I had no means, nor mechanism to defend myself because, I had already been labeled incompetent. This label reactivated what my relative whom I lived with when I was a child had labeled me, inadequate!

I finished the practicum without any encounter. I wish I had the strength to tell my previous team that did not allow me the opportunity that I am a woman whom they might have perceived differently, that I was a strong motivated woman who never wanted defeat whatsoever. Other times, I wanted to inform these people that "they should have asked me first where I came from before they began passing their own opinion about my accent"! When one works with immigrants and refugee women in this case, it is prudent you remember, you are dealing with people who are in pain and any kind of stigma just adds insult to injury. You are throwing darts at a fragile vessel that can break if you do not give it your support. No matter how long the person has been uprooted from their environment, the pain and the hurt are still there.

Through my experience as an immigrant woman and now a professional, I have come to view the immigration process similar to suffering a brain stroke. These immigrant women have to learn to walk, to talk again a language that could be understood by the host country, to move around the world again, and, probably the most difficult of all, is to learn to re-establish a sense of community. Csordas (1988) advocates for healing that is holistic for the immigrants, which may be important for people who have suffered war trauma. To him, a holistic healing approach includes all aspects of a person. This holistic healing is distinguished in three forms (1988):

> Physical healing; inner healing, in the case of mental problems, emotions and distress and also the healing of the suffering caused by such forces as evil spirits. He advocates that people who have suffered terrible war experiences need inner healing, which cannot be given in only one session or using simply one specific approach. He contends that such persons require "...comfort, acceptance, and understanding of the situation. And step-by-step [the person] can be brought back into the society, into work. And gradually [the person] gets back [their] own dreams, [their] motivation and [their] feeling that [there] is something and that [they are] alive. But during that time [they] suffer from those bad experiences, [they] need a kind of love and understanding. People don't react in the same way...but first, you give them comfort and tell them that the situation is not hopeless" (p.224).

Inner healing may gradually take place as the community immigrants come to live in demonstrated support. When there is a feeling of support and love, the traumatized person will gain strength to manage their depression and the nightmares of the past traumas. An essential aspect of the relief from the inner healing is also demonstrated by the trust where one feels a sense of belonging and of being accepted by their employers, colleagues and society as a whole.

SECTION IV

SERVICE PLANNING AND POLICY IMPLICATIONS

-❖-

In this section, I am giving the voice to African Women Immigrants. Through my story and other African Immigrant Women, we share what we think should be considered in the process of caring for us. The previous stories are testimonies of survival coping mechanisms which helped us to navigate the hardships of our pre and post immigration life challenges. We believe that, to be meaningful, any services provided to us must take into account our past, present socioeconomic context and aptitudes.

Do your best to know us

The last 50 years of barbaric civil wars in many African countries saw human rights violations perpetrated against the general population. Consequently a high percentage of the population may display symptoms of PTSD and other types of emotional disturbance.

The approaches these societies are familiar with in healing from their traumas, are cultural and traditional methods which include religious prayers, using traditional healers and herbal treatment. The Western model of psychotherapy is based on individual therapy rather than holistic therapy of dealing with everyone in the family. Focusing on the individual rather than the family or clan unit is an unfamiliar concept to the African women.

The challenges facing these immigrants and refugees in their new societies are complex and their needs are great. Besides facing enormous cultural and language differences, AIR women contend with limited programs that are culturally specific. Moreover, clinical studies show that rates of Post-Traumatic Stress Disorder (PTSD) among immigrant and refugee populations range from 39 percent and 100 percent (compared with 1 percent in the general population) while rates of depression range between 47 and 72 percent (Jaranson, James et al. 2004).

The impact of war trauma, social isolation and change in social status make acculturation difficult for this population. But also, the professionals who receive them when not familiar with the challenges of treating these people. In order to best respond to the needs of African clients, it is important to understand their unique experiences and circumstances. In assisting these women immigrant and refugees from troubled countries, the Canadian professional is likely to be dealing with even greater cultural discrepancies than found in other minority groups. Knowledge must be gained in each instance from the client and from background sources about the historical, spiritual, and socio-political realities from which these women come.

Unfortunately, failure to appreciate the significance of diverse cultural realities of the self in relation could result in serious misunderstanding, such as assuming standards for Western, middle-class, women, as the universal normative of assessing these women, while ignoring or devaluing unfamiliar religious attitudes, communal or tribal affiliations, and ancestral lineages or aesthetic and traditional practices that hold existential meaning for these women (Masinda & Kambere, 2008).

As I mentioned earlier, when traumatized individuals request assistance in dealing with their past experiences and their effects of sleep disturbance, isolation, and hypervigilance, the immediate intervention involves supporting them by listening to their experiences and attempting to normalize their feelings. In some cases, this type of debriefing at least provides immediate relief and assurance that someone is listening.

It is important that when professionals begin to work with this population, they need to understand how these people have been affected by the above outlined factors. To them cultural and spiritual beliefs prescribe how individuals account for life's circumstances. How African women explain the cause of trauma has consequences for psychosocial adjustment. For professionals and other persons helping these people, it is vital to persevere in holding these women by their hands, correcting them with gentleness, a sign that you care and you feel their pains. The most obvious and most overly looked thing about perseverance is that it only makes sense if you're heading in the right direction as the victim. For instance even after these women have been resettled and happily integrated, they still remain vulnerable to future stress, as was experienced by the exacerbation of symptoms that followed the Oklahoma City bombing and the September 11 broadcast as explained by Kinzie (2006).

This script resonates with my own personal experiences of arousal upon arrival to Canada and also 22 years after the coup d'état in my country. One such incident happened on May 2, 2008 when my husband and I visited Disney Land in the United States. I recall when we were being driven by a friend who had come to meet us at Disney Land Hotel and suddenly, we started hearing fireworks noises that sounded like gunshots. My heart sunk. I tried to compose myself, but the panic continued because this reminded me of the ugly experience that I had over twenty years before. In other words, it is clear that people who have had previous trauma, especially if the violence has some association to past experiences, even the slightest reminder may trigger some past memories!

The victims of past traumas have a long journey to work on their emotional and psychological healing in conjunction with professional help. In my long journey dealing with my past, I have realized that health bonds with other people are what get us to deeper levels of healing. They understand where you are coming from and gone through. As a survivor of pre-post-trauma, I understand the fears and the anxieties that come with trying to build close friendships with acquaintances and professionals alike.

Unlike some of the war trauma victims that I have met, I was fortunate to have mentors who believed in me and did everything they could to encourage me to seek a career that might help other immigrants. These mentors and acquaintances encouraged me to focus on new life that I feel has become very therapeutic for me personally as I work with people who have been traumatized. Reaching where I am truly took a formidable task of long years, with a desperate desire to have a circle of friendship, a habitation for healing, a place of mutual speaking and listening, learning and teaching, supporting and being supported, giving, and receiving unconditional love. When I finally found these circles of friendships, we created a network where we could share our stories, build intimacy and learn healthy communication without being intimidated.

As I look back to my early life in exile both in Congo and in Canada, I realize that I could not have walked this journey alone without women who believed in me and encouraged me to take the root of my career where I could share my personal story with others. We are social beings who have to lean on each other as we seek healing. We surely need each other! We need our community; we need friends with whom we can talk about our struggles. Yes, it is scary to think of laying out all your past burdens for others to see.

The only solace is to remove our masks, come out of hiding, disentangle ourselves from the addictions we may have used to replace our pains and learn how to tell others the truth about what we have been through. That way, we can be helping ourselves and others who read our stories about our experiences. I have learnt that speaking about my personal experience has become a stepping stone toward coming to terms with my past- and toward breaking its power over my life. The fact that the suffering of the women in this script were kept in the dark in the first place was not helping in any way until after we all got together to share what we each had been burdened with.

The healing process described here does not mean that only ethnic professionals are experts in working with their community. Education in trauma counseling and awareness on how to deal with people that have had trauma is essential. I recall a moment in my first days working with this group after I had just finished my social services certificate. One African woman came to me for counseling after being dismissed from her nutrition program at one of the colleges in Vancouver. She was in her last semester to get her diploma in nutrition when she was expelled from the program. Throughout the school program, she had experienced some rough time with her instructor, according to what she shared with me. I do not want to elaborate the situation, but her class work ended when the professor had slapped her in the face in front of the rest of the class. Despite all the legal help from the university council she had sought related to the matter, nothing worked in her favor-she was simply expelled from the program.

The woman came to me crying after she had tried all possible council members, but all in vain! I was not prepared to hear her story because I had not yet gone through my own cleansing. Her story was a re-visitation of my own past trauma. I did not know how to handle such complicated matters. As the woman narrated her own story, it took me back a hundred miles into the dungeon of my own past trauma. While she was describing the graphic details of her abuse throughout the course, I began to break out into a drenching sweat and eventually ceased hearing what she was talking about. Somehow, her descriptions of her experience triggered an excruciating string of the ugly memories of my own as if someone had thrown in a videotape recording of every horrid detail of my own past.

Due to my lack of knowledge in the field of trauma counseling, self-care was not an option. I decided to carry on with my prior arranged engagements without reflecting on what I had just absorbed. I chose to rush through the session for my next appointment. To be honest with you, it was the worst mistake that I have ever made. I got on the bus to be at the meeting that I had in the community, but short minutes later on the bus, my head started spinning. I could not understand what was going on. I felt nauseated. I totally felt out of place. I held on to the bus rails, but everything around seemed chaotic. After thirty minutes on the bus going through the experience, I decided to take the same route back to the office to inform my supervisor of what had just happened to me.

It is through my interaction with the women and some bit of study about trauma experience that I have had some understanding about what was happening with me, reliving my past trauma! Treating the consequences of war trauma in immigrant and refugee women, and other minority groups is not always an easy process, but it is also complicated by several factors. Among those factors includes the treatment of such problems, which are often related to past abuse as well as to current adverse conditions or reminders. The solace is that professional workers and community helpers from these ethnic groups are all still in the process of learning how to deal with victims of trauma and what self-care means as has been documented in many publications.

Take seriously the power of social connections

It is the social support that immigrant women receive from their new community that could bring a stable mind as they settle in their new host country. When they receive rejection and criticisms from their employers or are judged by the way they look, dress or speak, this can be an added trauma, thus making it difficult for a new immigrant person to fully integrate in their new society. It is the support and guidance that they receive that would give them a sense of belonging.

Social connection can lead to a long lasting relationship; it can also be a healing process for people who are isolated or have had troubled experiences. It is my assumption through my personal experience of isolation that the obvious healing resource available to human beings is social support and social connections, which seem to be the most powerful in protecting against mental and physical health problems. Social isolation, lack of feeling connected to people, or not having trusted people to interact with could worsen mental and physical health outcomes. The most important aspect of helpful social support is those individuals' trust and being open with people in their social support network. It is easier said than done. When I first came to Canada, it was not easy to simply connect with people.

I tried to wave at anybody on the bus who looked African, none of these approaches worked! In other cases where I could have gotten support, it was very difficult to trust people, with fear that anybody could be a spy for the country I was running from. Through my interaction with many immigrants and refugees from the continent of Africa, women have shared with me how they often struggle to trust others in their community if they fear that their private information will be shared publically, by those who have not had similar experiences.

As I widened the scope of my social and professional network, I found that this was a delusion that I had to remove from my mind and I began to open up. As I have shared in previous chapters, it was through my socialization and sharing with professionals at Hastings Adult Learning School, that I was able to get into the social work profession. If I had kept myself with this delusion of fearing everyone, I would not have had the opportunity of getting connected with professionals who envisioned things from a broader perspective. When the teachers heard me share my experience, they encouraged me to join social work so I could be a mentor to my fellow immigrants. It is obvious that everybody who has had some sort of trauma needs people in their lives to help them get through the tough times of settling in some places that sometimes may not be welcoming (Kozak, 2010). We are social creatures who need each other and we can be highly resilient, and able to withstand the most horrific of circumstances and resume life once the trauma is over if we find a supportive social network (Kitchen, Williams, Chowhan, 2012). When you are in a new environment it takes hard work before one establishes some sort of connections; but once you get integrated, it takes so little to connect, to let another know that he/she isn't alone, and that an experience is shared.

Social connection is a human tendency that does not only affect immigrants, but anyone new in a place. The challenge of social connection can lead to new opportunities or bring growth in one way or another, especially when you are in a new culture. It is the connection that you find in the community around that gives you the hope to feel connected and accepted. An example is the experience of one student among a group of American university students who went for their practicum at Rwentutu Community School in Western Uganda, as part of their overseas experience. This is what one student shared about her experience trying to find her identity in the new community:

> We have come to love Kasese and in general I would say we feel settled in. We can walk around town on our own, we have made friends at the local market who sell us fruits and vegetables every Sunday without hiking the prices up (like they do for foreigners, especially white people because it is generally assumed that we have more money and can afford to pay more), and we have made a fair number of friends in Kasese who stop by our house every so often just to check in on us and make sure we are doing okay. No matter where you are in the world, it is so good to have the company of friends. I don't think you can really understand the beauty of friendship until you are somewhere completely unfamiliar and you find people who care enough about you to check in on you, invite you to dinner at their home, or just tag along with you to watch a soccer game. To know that in the small amount of time we have been here, we have made friends who care about us and who we could call on if we needed anything really means a lot to us. It makes us feel like we belong instead of just being the visitors (Kathy: An American Practicum student at Rwentutu community school, July 4, 2010).

You cannot feel complete if you leave in a community where people are not welcoming. The above quote is from an American student, who is well advanced in the way things work in the Western World, but her words resonate with what most of the AIR women have been struggling with as they settle in their Canadian society.

It is in this sharing that strengths can pass from one heart to another, simply as a result of the connection. Evidently, what is communicated is caring, which eventually brings a sense that together "we" can get through whatever is happening around us. Through the togetherness, there is mutual understanding of building a world that needs each other.

Take a holistic approach

Although my focus is mainly on the immigrant and refugee women from the continent of Africa, when it comes to traumatic experiences, each culture suffers the effects of catastrophic situations differently. Refugee women flee for their lives from their countries of origin with scars of mothers having been raped by their own children, as women have identified in their narratives. Women witness their dead relatives left unburied, they witness their own sons killing their fathers; these are all inversions of social norms and perversions of accepted values constituted by destruction of the social order that undermine a coherent sense of life and meaning, thus in itself a traumatic experience only known to the bearers. Mollica (2007) has the following findings:

> Those around us, including our families, neighbors, doctors, and therapists, may know little about the curative value of social activities. More significantly, since they have no knowledge of the inner working of our minds and are not directly in touch with our traumatized world, only the most empathetic of our relatives and neighbors will realize what is needed and thereby be able to help. These people may in fact be afraid that the traumatized person's situation is hopeless and nothing can really be done (p.189).

The above statement demonstrates the holistic approach that is needed when dealing with people who have been traumatized in one way or another. After these AIR women have been traumatized by the events of war, it is difficult for them to develop any trust in anybody. One woman's narrative explains what living in fear after resettlement affects many of the victims of war trauma:

> Well it is always so raw, it is always in the present, you can't really shake it off. One of the things that were so hard for me was to develop trust. I had hard time trusting people, I thought people could be nice, but they could also be animals, you know. So I was really insecure that you know I had hard time trusting anyone. Oh the other thing is fear, I guess fear goes when you don't trust, there is fear of the unknown. And then the other thing is not to be able to enjoy anything. You always feel guilty

you know, you think, why did I survive I mean there are so many people who didn't survive and they were good people and they didn't survive and then trying to make meaning to what was happening, you know looking back like you know, I couldn't even go to the restaurant and enjoy myself. I could be eating in a nice restaurant and then it would just come back all of a sudden and then I would just begin crying (int #1., 2008).

After going through the horrendous experiences of war trauma, how can the host communities begin to understand the effects of the social dislocation inflicted by this kind of war on these women? It is only through a listening ear, from tender heart and an understanding of how war not only deprives the innocent victims of their well-being, but destroys their psychological and emotional being. Unfortunately, the African women find that it is an illusion that they had in mind before they finally got resettled in Canada. There are biases that have intervened and societies such as Canada have treated these newcomers unequally, favoring immigrants and refugees of one country or ethnic group over those of another as described by (Agnew, 2007).

These women had beautiful dreams and ambitions for themselves and their families, but they are usually shattered by the political instabilities in their countries of origin. As a result of these insecurities, these women are forced to leave their familiar surroundings, hoping to find new horizons, new hopes and security. The African refugees do not leave their countries of birth because of seeking good fortunes, but most of them are fleeing for their lives. When they arrive in their new country of destination, they have false hopes and delusions of finding green pasture on the other side of the continent. The intensification of day to day rush is largely another product of added stress (Orphana, Lemyre & Gravel, 2009) as one woman put it:

I never knew how tough it was [here in Canada]. Where I come from you are surrounded by so many people and you have got so much help that you never realized just how tough it is. So, yeah, life is stressful. So, I have to say, I have never been so stressed in my life than I have been in this country. I think my life has regressed rather than improved since coming to this country. You know you end up being [helpless], because you are so stressed, life is so stressful (Interview F 6#: Creese, 2009, p. 194).

It is the guidance from people who have walked our path, who understand our journeys and struggles that we have gone through, that can provide the social instruments of healing which are equally relevant for people who have seriously had health threats such as cancer, stroke or heart attack (Mollica, 2006). Given the right tool, we will dance with the flow and people will marvel at where we got the resiliency.

Construct smooth paths: the mainstream services

One woman asked me during my interaction with her, two months after she had arrived in the country.

> How can I trust you when I know that you have not had similar experiences as mine? I have found it difficult to go to these Canadian counselors to talk about my personal experience when I know that they know nothing about what it means to see a man rape you in front of your children. What strength will they give me when I am the one who has had horrible experience of sleeping on the roadside begging for food while my children are watching me stand by the road as a beggar? Do they even know where we come from and what problems we come with? I can talk to that person who knows what it means by being in a refugee camp, what it means by coming to a country where you start life a fresh, where you have no relative to support you in your journey of being a refugee in Canada (field notes, 2006).

People who have had prior traumatic experiences are already wounded and carry with them images that are invisible to the social network or even professionals. Developing trust in their new society usually takes time. For instance, Bryant & Harvey (2000) point out that "It is common for people who have suffered unresolved traumatic experiences before the recent trauma to be confronted with the recent stressor and a resurgence of the earlier memories.

For example, a woman who survived a recent motor vehicle accident had seen her mother commit suicide 20 years earlier. Soon after the motor vehicle accident, she began experiencing severe posttraumatic stress symptoms, relating both to the motor vehicle accident and to her mother's death" (p. 140). This description is consistent with what most immigrant and refugee women in this script have shared. It also reflects my own experience when the community nurse came to my house and found me totally isolated and depressed. She found me at a point where I never wanted to entertain any discussion from any one I did not know. She found me at a point where I was immersed in my own tormented mind, not wanting any "intruders" to come to my created "comfort zone". Even hearing noise by my own children was like slapping me in the face because I was totally engraved in my pain of the past.

The community nurse visited me one sunny afternoon and found me isolated and not interested in entertaining anybody. The nurse I believe was doing what she was trained to do. She found me laying on the couch in my basement. When you are in such a state of mind, you do not want to interact even with your family members. Your children can fear to approach you fearing they may annoy you. This is what had happened to me that afternoon; my children couldn't reach me. One of them took the opportunity after seeing a visitor around, came crawling around me; I am sure this was the only way he wanted to be around his mother to find out what was happening, although he could not articulate anything to me. I felt like he was pulling my brain from my skull. I spanked the boy on his thigh in the presence of the nurse. The nurse freaked out and was shocked to see the kind of behavior I displayed in her presence. Not wanting any interference from my son or the community nurse, I felt like being choked by these two people's presence.

No professional had ever visited me nor had I had an opportunity to have someone with whom I could share my emotional trauma I was struggling with at the time. Was this some kind of psychological trauma I was going through at the time? I believe so. The nurse was not informed of my own internal turmoil I was going through either. Instead, she informed me that in Canada people don't spank children. Did I even want to hear what she tried to explain to me, since she had no idea what I was struggling with? Was this the time for her to begin lecturing me about the Canadian way of parenting when I was dealing with this internal turmoil? It was our first time to meet and what I needed at the time was someone to get into my shoes, hold my hand and say "I know where you are. I know what you are going through, come along with me and I will show you the way out of this emotional turmoil you are experiencing." Easier said than done!

One woman shares her experience as below:

Yeah, it does help you that you are safe, it is very hard to share it, what you went through. I didn't feel like I got the support in general, but support in terms of talking about it, or dealing with it, no. But I remember a time when I was really, really very depressed and I had to see a counselor. I was really traumatized and then the counselor told me to do some kind of you know, imagine myself in front of an ocean (laughter), I was like you are kidding me (Int. 1, 2008).

This woman did not see the need of seeking help until she was overwhelmed by the emotions and then she did seek help. Unfortunately she felt that the professional was trying to remind her to go back to her old situation which she describes as an ocean of some sort. Rosenbloom & Williams (2002), contend that:

...experiences of trauma shake the very foundation of [women's] being, including that [individual's] sense of safety, trust, control, self-worth, and connection with oneself and others. Traumatic events shatter illusions about how safe the world really is and how much control any individual has over his or her life (p.119).

For most survivors, the more obvious results of injury don't even compare to the relational damage that can last far into old age even after the situation is long gone. For instance Kinzie et al (2002) identify the effects of secondary traumatization from the tragic events of September 11, 2001. Their findings reveal that an ethnically diverse group of refugees who had prior trauma in their native war torn countries, had the greatest deterioration in their subjective sense of safety and security. Their findings confirm what most of the AIR women with whom I have shared my story are likely to develop, if professionals and the host country do not meet their needs with understanding of their prior experiences. Even though these women might not have had direct encounters with shocking levels of traumatic experiences, they have nevertheless come to fear for their lives in one way or another because of the fact that they have taken flight and come into exile, which is in most cases a traumatic experience on its own (Polanco-Roman, & Miranda, 2013 ; Edge, Newbold & McKeary, 2014; Blackwell, 2005).

Help family reunification

Family separation is another torture that women have to deal with when they finally settle, especially if there are family members, such as children, spouses, parents, and/or other family members, who remain in highly concentrated conflict areas. Such memories of where these family members are and how they are living can be a source of significant suffering and worry. When these issues are combined with experiences of isolation caused by a lack of support network in the new host countries, it becomes traumatizing for an immigrant and refugee woman. In most cases, the impact of the separation from their familiar surroundings, usually cause a lot of mental health problems to these victims (Wasik, 2006; Dossa, 2004; Judith, 1997).

The most pressing concerns for refugees who have found protection in Canada or elsewhere is for their family left behind, either in refugee camps or with family members who were kind enough to take custodial care of their children. Many get to their countries of resettlement after they have had their husband or child killed; some their houses burned down, and others their family members imprisoned. Many women make it to countries of refuge with only some of their children or hardly knowing where the rest are. The process of locating some of their relatives could take a period of more than three years or even decades! Subsequently, the longer the separation, the slower the integration of the refugees into the new society and often part of their family is still missing.

Parents separated from children often suffer from depression as it was in my case. When these women are seen in public places, such as churches or malls, all the time they are listening to internal stimuli about their own problems regarding their kids. Like one woman said:

> So when I think about my kids I just have to take it by myself. I sit here and listen to my music and cry...I say, 'I wish I was there with my mum,' or I cook, or I go outside, you know.... It's really hard" (Focus group, Jane Francis, 2009). Another one states: "I just wish we could get the counselling. And I just wish, like so that may be even we could just move away from that focus to say, oh African women, when they come overseas. They could move away from that and just focus to look for what is the problem. What is needed to be done you know. And I guess even

the counselling should be done by African people, not even the White Canadians…it pains me to see an African family [living separate lives]. It is not like the culture (interview F22).

Also, during the long uncertain period when they do not know when their children may arrive, people do not know from one month to the next how many bedrooms they will need, leading to instability. One worker described it like this:

They're in this in-between space, knowing that their family is coming but not knowing when, but needing to find housing. So it's always temporary and that seriously affects the capacity to be stable in housing…One woman got into a co-op, then sponsored her family, and anticipating their arrival she moved out. She's now in a market situation, but it's already been months that they are arriving 'tomorrow,' so that really affects where people live and how they are housed…Now she's ready to look in the paper every month for a 3-bedroom apartment that will accommodate the family on her salary…it's really complicated!(Jane Francis, 2009).

Family separation not only prevents families from integrating and building assets together; it is also costly. For example, because sponsors are separated from their legal dependents, they must maintain two households (here and overseas), possibly for several years. Phone cards constitute another cost. In addition, Africans are disproportionately asked to provide DNA samples to prove family relationships, which are time consuming and expensive. Meanwhile, security clearances and medical checks expire and have to be repeated, causing further cost and delays. Finally, processing times for family sponsorship vary significantly by region, with Africa by far the slowest (CCR, 2004).

Women flee their countries because of atrocities. It is usually abrupt and they leave without knowing where their children are or even their spouse! In my case, at least I had enough time to plan my move. I prepared to leave our first child behind, with hope that he would follow us when we got resettled. At that time the child was only four years. When I arrived in exile in Congo, all the emotional pains and guilt crowded my mind. Life became even worse than when I was in the war zone. There was no single time that I had peaceful sleep without thinking about my son. He was only three years! Quite frankly, I never enjoyed my meals during the four years this child was in Uganda. There were times when I cried and had nightmares about him. The complexities of beginning a new life in the new country without my son and learning about the new country's legal system, about family or immigration law compounded with the loss of identity from my country of origin had a major effect on my life.

I do not know how my husband handled this whole ordeal. I will only talk for myself about my own experience as a mother and a wife in this situation. Even though I had my husband around, the way I needed to deal with the shame and disappointment of leaving our child behind could not give me the strength to regain control, connection, and meaning in order to live a healthier, fuller life in this country. I disassociated myself from reality, not even wanting to make connections with people around me. I do not know whether I was aware of what I was doing to myself, and I still have no answer.

When you disassociate or develop a sense of detachment spacing out, there are feelings of numbness, and I was not even aware of what was going on. Furthermore was the inability to concentrate, which manifested itself as difficulty in listening to any conversation my husband brought up regarding coping mechanism in the new culture, thus only being distracted and preoccupied by the thoughts of my son's welfare, the only thing I cherished. I "idolized" my miseries. Life was meaningless. When you internalize your pains, there is hardly any moment that you will think about productive activities or socialize with people who could help out. Such disassociation triggers a lot of memories about the good times that one had. It may lead also to self-damaging thoughts and indulging in unacceptable social behaviors such as drugs.

Use and combat the strain of nostalgia

There are many factors that affect immigrants and refugees from countries that have had instabilities. They are likely to be vulnerable from the get-go and on a day-to-day basis. Most of them encounter in their host country relentless economic, cultural, and social obstacles, such as stressors that may worsen their vulnerability to the risks involved. Most of them develop a psychological coping mechanism of nostalgia. Nostalgia is described as a coping strategy for alleviating acculturative stress and for contributing to successful acculturation patterns, such as integration.

First of all, nostalgia has different definitions, such as personal nostalgia, defined as "a sentimental longing for the past" (The New Oxford Dictionary of English, 1998, p. 1266) and historical nostalgia defined as a sentimental longing for a historical period of which one may or may not have been a part. These two definitions describe the participants in this script. For immigrants who come from war trauma and find a very unfriendly environment may find nostalgia a coping mechanism.

What I know from my own personal and professional experiences, some immigrant women and men who come as professionals and find the environment not friendly, especially when their academic credentials are often not recognized in their new host country, they usually have a longing of wanting to go back. They get stressed due to the cumulative nature of economic, cultural, and social predicaments encountered in the host country, especially where they cannot provide for their families as they used to do when they were in their good times. These stressors can be exacerbated by conditions inherent in the immigrant's society of origin, such as lack of accepted education, leading them to do menial jobs at a minimum wage.

More generally, the stress stems from both and often conflicting requirements of participation in two cultures. Each time they are pressed with negative experiences around employment or lack of support network of friends, they find themselves developing symptoms of "negative" nostalgia, such as being sad or lonely. The negative symptoms that are commonly experienced by women include homesickness, which is mainly a psychological aspect where people will develop some anxiety attack or depression (van Tilburg, Vingerhoets, & van Heck, 1996) and even wanting to go back to the countries that they ran from so that they could simply go and die there.

I was like that. As indicated earlier, each time I felt lonely in my two bedroom basement, the only thing I thought of was "I wish I could go back home to the country I ran from, so that I could go and die there, despite the problems I was running from." Additionally, nostalgia pertains to many more objects than homesickness (Wildschut, Sedikides, Arndt, & Routledge, 2006). Mine was not homesickness; it was social connections that I missed in the first place. The sense of worthlessness was insurmountable. I missed my family! There were times I really needed my mother to be around me and bring me food.

I came with my four boys and the baby was only five months. It is customary in my culture that in each case when a married daughter gets a new baby, the mother sends relatives or young siblings with gifts to visit their sister. In my case, I was in Canada with a five months old baby who would never have the opportunity of these traditional moments. I longed for that moment where my mother would send my young sister or relatives to come and visit me whenever I had a new child. I was totally lost in my new country with this new baby I never have such an opportunity to celebrate his arrival with my relatives. All this brought a lot of negative feelings that Davis (1979) talks about in his research when he found that participants associate the words, old times, and yearning more frequently with nostalgia than with homesickness.

I missed momentous occasions such as religious festivals, traditional weddings, and family visits which are common in the African cultures, where a family member simply visits without making any appointments. It is evidenced in the women's narratives in this script that many of the women's negative levels of nostalgia was when they were in a bad mood especially after hearing bad stories from back home about their family members or when discriminated at work by their fellow workers; such incidents brought about nostalgic feelings.

There are a few incidents in this narrative where some of the women say that nostalgic feelings contributed substantially to their successful integration by promoting psychological health and bolstering interpersonal adequacy; in my case, it was totally different. For some women who are resilient, these experiences are both personally and culturally meaningful. Developing positive attitudes about current and past nostalgia has helped some of the immigrant women navigate more smoothly the stressful experiences of their existence in their new home country.

How can women experience positive nostalgic feelings and be healed from the scars of the past when these groups continue to face rejections as opposed to the illusions they came with from refugee camps? One woman has the following comments:

> Any place we went for a job they will make this racist remarks because they will make us feel too bad. Sometimes I cried and I said you know I prefer to go back home than to stay here because the racism is too much. Even at work, you know, you say let me stay, you come to work and two of us get the same [job]. Like I remember me and this East Indian lady, she did not know how to read; we went there, she got the job before me because the color

is not the same. It makes me feel sick. I was so sick that day when I came [home] I said oh my God, I wish I could go back home" (focus group # 1).

Another woman laments:

I mean like, let's face it, if you are a black person your chances of survival in this system is not as high as that of Canadian born, even if you are Canadian born and your skin is black. You will always face discrimination, racism that is. It's real as natural. You know, it's like a natural thing, it's a natural phenomenon. Like you go look for a job, and you know you are well qualified [these are things that bring negative feelings and longing of going back to our countries of origin] (interview M 45: Creese, 2009, p. 144).

The difficulties these women are faced with in their integration process into their new Canadian society are reminders of longing to go back to their countries of origin. To these women, integrating successfully into Canadian society is very difficult because they cannot find good jobs that utilize their prior training and education; and the institutional racist policies compounded with the unacceptance of the host society and its reaction to this group all become a barrier for them to fully integrate. They are often told "you need Canadian experience", but no one is willing to give them an opportunity to develop the Canadian experience.

Several of the women had reported such occurrences as they tried to engage in meaningful activities such as employment. This was the only way they could make themselves happy and be productive members of society. They only get shocked to see that they are not accepted by the very system that was supposed to help them integrate. The following quote explains how the system racializes immigrant women in relation to work experience: How do we have experience as an immigrant? This person is an immigrant and you say do you have any experience in Canada, eh? (Focus group # 1, 2008). Most of the women participants in this study had high expectations given by United High Commission for Refugees in Africa before resettling in Canada. These expectations are only shattered by lack of understanding on the receiving end. Another woman laments:

I was studying there and I should be a teacher and my husband should be a doctor, but here to find that job, we can't find it. It is really hard, the government of Canada needs to change that because we don't like that situation and even when we go and find a job, they need to see if we know good English. The color that we have as black people becomes a negative aspect for us combined with lack of good English; it is tough for us" (Focus group #1, 2008).

They have segregation for color, for language, segregation for countries, especially for us who speak French, we speak English, we speak Swahili, we speak Kirundi, we speak four languages, but we can't find good jobs we want to do here. Even we speak French we can't go and teach in French schools. It is very hard (Focus group #1, 2008).

When these participants cannot find jobs, they feel rejected and disillusioned by the lack of acceptance to use their prior training. One woman whose disappointment had made her not worthy staying in the country had this to say:

...when confronted by all these injustices] and I remember my country, and I remember what happened, and I think, if there is no war there, I could simply go back. I live here because there, there is no peace otherwise, I could go back" (Focus group #1, 2008).

The conditions of war, abandonment of cultural values and loss of status are not the inevitable legacy of many African immigrant and refugee women's past. When an individual woman becomes self-aware, there is the potential for insight. With insight comes the potential for altered behavior.

With altered behavior comes the potential to diminish the trans-generational passage of dysfunctional or destructive ideas and practices. As a society, we cannot develop true insight without self-awareness. Enduring socio-cultural changes in racism, misogyny and maltreatment of refugee women cannot occur without institutional and cultural insight and the resulting altered institutional and cultural behavior. The challenge for the new Canadian generation that is going to work with these groups is to understand the dynamics and realities of the human living groups in a way that can result in group insight, which, inevitably, will lead to the understanding of that society; they must change their institutionalized ignorance and maltreatment of people who have suffered past trauma such as those who come from war traumatic situations (Kambere, 2004; Creese, 2009; Masinda & Kambere, 2008; Dossa, 2002).

Most of the new immigrants are prone to indirect discrimination which involves earlier decisions that set the stage for subsequent discriminatory consequences. An example is policies about the rights of immigrants, which render long-term upward mobility virtually impossible. Direct discrimination involves easily observable and inferior work or living conditions for immigrants. For example, immigrants suffer from a higher unemployment rate than natives in every Western European country (Pettigrew, 1998) and newly-arrived immigrants are highly likely to experience downward occupational mobility (e.g., working on jobs that are below their educational or skill level in Canada (Creese, 2009; Masinda & Kambere, 2009) as I did when I newly migrated.

These factors contribute to acculturative stress in the receiving society, but also include "social hardships" such as stereotypes, prejudice, and discrimination of these groups. It has been argued by many psychologists that immigrants and refugees when they encounter this constellation of negative affectivity symptoms, they resort to nostalgia (Brown & Humphreys, 2002; Volkan, 1999). Turning to nostalgic memories of their past cultural heritage might offer resources for staving off a seemingly uninspiring present and future in the host country.

From these women's narratives, it is obvious that the strain of nostalgia has taken a huge toll on them. In fact these women are taken by surprise from their narratives when their emotions are crushed by what they experience as they seek employment and other fulfilling opportunities. Their disillusionment causes some of them to become despondent and believe that there is no hope to survive in their new country, thus thinking of going back to their troubled countries they ran from.

Some of them will remain with scars of whether life back home would have been better than the illusions of being in first world society. Especially, it is very difficult for these women not knowing whether they should identify themselves with the new society that does not seem to accept them, or continue to identify themselves with their old societal and cultural values. I will explain their predicament in the next chapter.

Help individual construct healthy new identities

Identity could mean a lot of different things to different people at different times. When one develops a sense of identity, they feel they belong to certain group of people or accepted in the group. As a result this gives them the autonomy to claim what they feel belongs to them, or what they feel they have as a legal obligation to identify themselves with. We are social beings who identify ourselves by virtue of where we belong and where we are accepted. When people feel acknowledged and perceived by people around them, it gives a sense of worthiness and feeling of being a member of society/group whose values and attributes are for the betterment of society. For these women the integration process in their new home country demonstrates how they construct their lives in the new country as pointed out:

I think for me, the most difficulty has been finding your place within the community, as to where are you in this community, are you really a member of this community? Do you really feel that you belong; do you really see a future for yourself? You know those kinds of things. Of course finding what you really want to do and being happy in it, the right job, and employment [is what makes you feel you belong]. I will say the opportunity to highly [develop] my skills. I think it is difficult finding a place you can actually be able to utilize your skills and excel. Different barrier or maybe perceived ones, but I also think it is about how to be established or a network (Mapendo, Focus group 2003) she was 8 years in Canada, with an American M.A.

Another immigrant woman recounts her own interpretation and frustrations of how the system of "others" places her in a different bracket of identity. She maintains that:

For me, who has been here for about three years now, I think that there is no sense of belonging. I feel there is no future for me. I struggle with this every time to overcome this situation. But the more I struggle the more it becomes harder and harder.

One thing is that you cannot find a job, you don't know where to start, and you don't know where these connections and networking are (Kathy was 3 years in Canada by the time of this interview, 2003; Sudanese M.A.).

To these AIR women, belonging carries many connotations. It means having a strong connection with other people as well as an establishment of job opportunities. From a psychosocial perspective it is worth noting that social boundaries play a huge role in individual people's lives. The social disconnection that AIR women experience in their new country like what I experienced in Congo places us in a different category.

I did not speak the same language as the women that I met in Congo although we were all Africans. This placed me in another category of people who were identified as "others". I was identified as a refugee woman from Uganda no matter the ethnic connection we all had due to the color of our skin. We still remained disconnected from each other in that context because we did not share the same language. This identity placed me in another category of being "an outsider who came from Uganda." With this social comparison referring to me as a refugee woman on the block from the main social group with whom I lived distanced me from the rest of the community.

Social identity is evidenced in social groups that have shown more power, prestige or status than others who are different from them, such as the immigrant and refugees. My experience living in two cultures has made me become aware that members of a group will compare their own groups with others and determine the relative status of their own group. I am now cognizant through all these experiences of social identity that no matter whether you have a common bond of skin color, there is always a tendency for members of a group to distance themselves from membership of a group which does not share the same beliefs and ideas of their group and take more account of the beliefs and ideas of their social group.

The concept of social identity has been developed in social policy as it is useful to promoting an understanding of the collective social bond in responses to ethnic communities' needs. My own observations in both environments in my African culture and the Canadian society have been different. When I am with my Canadian friends, I am always asked tell me "where are you from, your skin complexion and accent inform me that you are either from Africa or Fiji". Such remarks are implications that my identity is questionable; therefore, I do not belong to the social group even though I might be socially connected to their network. This is reflective of what I experienced in my own African culture! I lacked the language command and was constantly asked where I was from, the same experience that has followed me even to this day here in Canada. Is this by coincidence or a matter of self-identification? This reflects us humans as social beings that will always have preferences of who we are and who are more closely related to us. With this experience, I have come to accept that even if I were in African countries, I would still be treated in a similar manner as I am in Canada due to the fact that we as humans-being social beings still have our own identities according to the values and norms that we hold.

When I lived in The Democratic Republic of Congo, then Zaire, I found myself being introduced as a "Ugandan refugee woman", whose husband was an MP even though we shared same skin color. I should say that the MP's wife "status" gave me some dignity among the local women, but did not give me identity. This means I lived among the community women who knew that my identity is "a Ugandan woman, not local woman like them!" Quoting Appiah 2005,p 64 in Agnew 2007, she points out:

> Identities arise in a 'structured field of relations' and are a consequence, not the cause, of conflicts. Cultural differences do not give rise to collective identities; rather, differences of identity are in many ways prior to those of culture. Identity writes, Appiah, is both who we are and what we are; that is, it incorporates a descriptive criteria such as race, gender, and sexuality but also a belief system that is associated with them.

This demonstrates that what we believe about our identity shapes everything we do and everything about us. In simplicity, if an individual believes that their worth is based on superficial things, you might find yourself living for someone else's approval, ambitious yet dissatisfied and even insecure and in many cases always feeling like a failure. But when we know the truth about our identity, we will get empowered to live a life of purpose, confidence and genuine love for others who are around us (Stanley 2008). The experience of my new identity gave me an understanding of who I was in this new country, especially the refugee status, and the role in constructing my new identity in Congo.

Agnew claims about new identities that people receive as they become immigrants, refugees or asylum seekers living in countries that are not their birth place. Thus, to Agnew (2007), experience is not the endpoint of our self, but the beginning of an exploration of the relationship between the personal and the social and therefore the political. I spoke English and most women and community members respected me for that. The only difference is that I was not within my own identity boundaries, and above all, I had the mark of "a Ugandan refugee woman on the block"!

Unfortunately even when the women have settled in what they call their new country of settlement, there is the sense of "what next" if I can't get integrated due to this identity issue? When you see them they have feelings of loneliness even though they may be in a group of other people. They are still identified as "others", meaning that they are not part of the main structure, when such critical identifications are brought up. These are tendencies that women encounter in their everyday social interactions with different people who are not from their own ethnic groups. When such reminders are brought up before they even settle in their new home, it leaves them with senses of alienation.

Yes, we all experience a number of tough moments and situations that temporarily or semi-temporarily shake the basis of our self-worth and identity; such may even diminish the meaning of our personal existence. Being reminded of "where are you from" is one of the most self-invalidating experiences, since everyone's life revolves around social relationships and self-concept. It is such a lonely and alienating experience of being identified as "other" a tendency that has become part of the women's daily occurrences which leaves them with questions of whether they really are welcomed in their new society.

It is a delicate issue from the person saying it even where there is no bad intention behind the question. Unfortunately, to the receiver, or the person being asked, it is a reminder that you have not yet arrived because you are still being identified as "other", especially if the one asking such a question does not understand what experiences you have passed through (Creese & Kambere, 2003).

The loneliness and personal questioning of "where are you from?" has been a question that women feel bring painful emotion and psychological feelings. One woman had the following to say as she encountered the occurrence of being asked "where are you from?"

With me when I meet people who continuously ask me where I am from. My response to them is do you have a problem with me? Don't I look like I am supposed to belong here?" I simply tell them, from Surrey. Others I also ask them, where are you from yourself? When I ask them, then they live me alone (Field notes, 2008).

Although the questioning may be good intentioned, after you have been exposed to an environment where such questioning had a negative connotation, even the very meaningful intentions are usually misinterpreted. It is only those who experience this feeling that know how deeply it can attack self-esteem.

Many psychologists and counselors have highlighted the psychological and emotional effects of feeling rejected by the very people you feel are supposed to support you. A range of psychological processes take place when they are in such a situation. There is the feeling of being denied access to the right to be and the right to feel at such moments. Similarly, there is also a feeling as though a part in you is slowly dying in pain. There begins to grow a process of doubting one's self-worth, and losing confidence and self-respect.

Eventually, the self-identity gets shaken, and we become unsure of who we are and what we are. We eventually lose sight of the meaning of life and become hopeless and drifting. More importantly when there are no people around that you identify yourself with there will be inescapable moments when one will feel non-existent. For instance in my situation, when I was consistently asked "where are you from and where is this accent from?" when in a room full of people, I experienced a sense of being rejected!

Some of us internalize our emotional pains; others use those same pains as a tool to focus on things in a more productive way, while others either cry by seeking a high power to give them the strength to deal with their past pains so that they can be able to face their tomorrow with a promising mind. With me, when such feelings and emotional cloudiness bombarded me, it was my faith in prayer that helped me to overcome some of these questioning.

However, even though the questioning was bothersome, when I look back, this gave me another way of looking forward. Being angry or internalizing my emotions could not help me either. I gained the confidence to help other women who did not have the opportunity to overtly express their pains, or who did not have a social network of women to share their frustrations as I have found through this script. I am ever grateful that even though I still find people who question my identity, this no longer bothers me; instead, I have gained strength to be able to talk to my fellow immigrant women with confidence and also educate my professional colleagues about the challenges of being identified as "other" without fear of how they will take my point of view and/or opinion.

Capitalize on people's gratitude

In the hardship of my life experiences as a refugee in another country, there were also blessings that came along. In Congo, I had this experience with a stranger who became my guardian angel each time I was in desperate need. This stranger gave a hand to a stranger despite our social location in a strange country. This old man whom I will call Kyabuli, (not his real name) came to my aid when I most needed it. When you are in a strange land and meet people who show that they care and demonstrate their support to you, there is always a positive attitude that develops, which makes one face another day with hope and determination.

Thankfully, I found such a man who was able to demonstrate his love to the refugee woman on the block who was desperately in need. Kyabuli understood my situation and was very empathetic in ways that only I, the teller of the story could explain. It is my experience that when one is faced with situations that seem to have endless roads, one needs motivation, encouragement and sympathy. The old man Kyabuli's compassion transcended lines of love, encouragement and humanity just to mention a few qualities that I saw in this old man.

Let me first demonstrate how this old man's compassion to people evolved. It is unfortunate that as I write this script, he has passed on. I learnt about his death about fifteen years ago. This old man had a unique heart for people who came to live in his community. In my professional approach while dealing with people with mental illness and also with victims of war trauma such as the participants in this study, many stories have been shared about how these women feel, when they meet someone who encourages them in their journey of the unknown.

This is reflective of how this old man gave a listening ear to me, even though he did not have the traditional counseling skills that are required in the Western approach when dealing with victims of war. The way this man held me and supported me would be considered non-scientific, and thus not considered as a skill that should be used when helping people in need.

However, in dealing with the African women, and looking at how this man's approach helped me, I have learnt to emulate his skill as I connect with my fellow refugee women. I learnt from my three guardian angels to be kind to other people. Specifically, the approach that Kyabuli used in dealing with my situation has given me a different perspective on how to deal with people that need a listening ear and a helping hand. This old man always came to my door when I was in tears. He was particularly interested in knowing where we came from and what we did before we came to live in his neighborhood. One simple word of, "how are you doing today?" made a difference in my life at the time.

I admired his unique way of how he simply did not want to be identified as someone who was well off among his people. My early work with immigrant and refugee women brought home the point that this man demonstrated as he dealt with me, a new person in the neighborhood. It is important when dealing with a new person to first develop a rapport as it is usually the case in any social contact with a person that is new to you. Kyabuli had his own unique way of developing a rapport to effectively engage me in meaningful discussions that made me open up. In doing this, he requested of my husband if he could teach him English at least once a week. My husband accepted to help him because he was a teacher so this was an easy way of keeping himself busy and also to get some connections with a local person. The old man showed humanitarian compassion to us refugees in the community. Although he was interested in learning English, he got to know us in a way that was beyond compassion.

There were times when Kyabuli showed up at my door carrying a tin of powdered [Nido] milk that only middle class people used. What else could I tell a man such as this angel that had no boundaries by even reaching out to a refugee family like mine? I simply said, "Thank you." I saw the power of God in this man. He never sat down nor said anything, but left immediately after handing me the milk. When I recall these incidents, I wonder whether it was the old man Kyabuli, or an angel from God. How could he have known that I was in my house in tears craving for Nido milk?

I never wanted to show my neighbors that I was desperate or in a state of need. I still had to maintain my dignity and I handled myself well in the community. I had never shared my desperation with anybody. I found a unique sense of humor in Kyabuli. His smile and presence was very therapeutic to this refugee woman. I felt a sense of peace that there was someone in the neighborhood that cared and was willing to go an extra mile and reached out to exercise his compassionate heart.

Even his smile meant a lot to this refugee woman in this strange country. He gave me hope to move on into the next day with courage. This attitude is what most refugee people expect to find when they come to a foreign country, with people who would accept them despite their social, political and religious backgrounds. Such hospitality helps the new person gain courage with hope that the future is promising. My connection with both Kyabuli and dada, the woman who helped me with Gisenyi business and the host mother all brought to me a sense of relief and hope. The host mother sheltered me when I could have been on the streets with my two children. I paid nothing in return, but she spoke words of encouragement that gave me hope that the sky is the limit.

Dada was there to help me establish some market vending business for our survival in this country. She became my voice where I could not speak the language as we crossed the border to Rwanda, and also to connect with other women vendors. Kyabuli saw the need of a pregnant woman on the block who looked isolated and needed a support network. These three individuals appeared in my life when I needed someone to help in my helplessness and hopelessness. All of them had unique ways that reflected meaning to a helpless situation. They kept speaking into my life words of encouragement in a spiritual way (Koenig, 2010). They spoke words of wisdom that came from really mature and caring people who knew life's circumstances. They kept telling me words that I really needed to hear! Amartian (2006) points out that "We all need people who will help us see the truth about ourselves and our lives. And we need to have the kind of relationships that don't break down when truth is spoken in love" (p.143).

I really needed people to speak words of truth and hope in my life. Indeed, these three individuals came at such a time when I wanted such truth to be spoken even though I did not know how, but I knew that people saw some potential in me! Although these three individuals spoke encouraging words, this did not mean that my problems were over. When circumstances that surround us become gloomy, it is very difficult to ever think that we can rise up and be above our pains. Amartian (2006) further points out that

...{when} in an airplane on a gray, dreary, rainy day, I am always amazed at how we can fly right up through the dark wet clouds, so thick that we can't see one thing out the window, and then suddenly rise above it all and have the ability to see for miles. Up there the sky is sunny, clear, and blue. I keep forgetting that no matter how bad the weather gets, it's possible to rise above the storm to a place where everything is fine (p.187).

The fact that my long life struggles seemed to have no end, it also became very difficult for me to ever think that I would ever be where I am today as I write this book, especially today as I sit in this massive ship, on a cruise ship to Alaska, United States. When the dark clouds of trials, struggles and or suffering roll in and settle on people's lives, so thick and heavy, it is easy to not bother to see what lies ahead of us. It is very easy to forget that there is a place of calm, light clarity, and peace that we can rise to (Amartian, 2006).

When people are in the midst of trouble, tragedy, loss or disappointments, it really hurts and in many instances, it is impossible to think beyond these pains. The only important things that people need when they are in despair is a support network. For me, these three identified people in this script redeemed me when I desperately needed them around me at the time of isolation and suffering.

Everyone needs people around when they feel a sense of despair or when their aspirations have been shattered. Too often, people despair and give up on what would have helped others if they had support. We all need to be supportive to those whom we feel are vulnerable, especially those who are displaced and trying to find meaning for their lives. Today, as I write this piece of information I am thrilled to read in the Vancouver Sun about the fruits of our labor that were remote in my mind, that came after many years when our struggles did not seem to make sense:

The Surrey-based organization Umoja Operation Compassion, headed up by Ugandan-born couple Amos and Edith Kambere, has partnered with the Surrey Pacific Academy, the Dunamis Education Society and an NGO in Uganda to establish an elementary school in that country. In addition to helping establish this school, Umoja has helped other members of the Diaspora engage with development in their countries of origin.

They recently assisted a Vancouverite of Kenyan origin who returned to his home region and constructed a well providing water for an entire village. This project was completed at the surprisingly low cost of $2500 (Vancouver observer, Jan.21, 2011).

These compliments and accomplishments go to the people that helped us in our struggles. "Dada, or sister" became a catalyst for me to find my potential in the new country Congo. She helped me reach places of opportunity although there were failures along the way; she encouraged me to cross over beyond border to explore avenues of business.

She became a friend after all despite the ordeals that we both had endured in our own different ways. Kyabuli became an angel who appeared to me in a timely manner as I was desperately in need of financial and emotional support. His smile and sense of humor brought a lot of hope to a refugee woman in a strange country, where she had nobody to call for help. If these two were not supportive and encouraging, I am not sure what would have happened.

Kyabuli showed a compassionate heart that was timeless. He, became an old man from whom I drew my emotional strength when I needed to pour my heart out to someone, a male figure when my husband had gone to fend for our family! The host mother did not hold back her love for strangers, but demonstrated a compassionate heart that had no limits. These three people came into my life when I really needed someone to pour out my frustrations to. They shared my pains as though they were theirs. They each played their different roles in my own life.

I really wished that this world lived without any wars that displace innocent women and children who become the victims at the end of the day. Even after taking a refugee to another country, the suffering and miseries do not end there. It is true to believe the fact that displacement and dislocation do not come to an end upon immigration, but may continue in the country of resettlement, which results in unnecessary suffering. I recall a time when I would lock myself in my small room and start yelling, crying and calling out to God to really save me and get me out of this situation or else my children would die for lack of Medicare and proper hygiene.

Despite the waiting for answered prayers, many times I saw breakthroughs in many different areas. There were times when I would see unexpected guests come from the capital city of Congo DRC and left me with money that would take me through the week. There were other times when God answered my prayers in unexpected ways where someone would come from the church group where I attended, and give me encouraging words, which I needed most!

Help folks unlock their hopes

I needed people to motivate me, but where could I have found them when there were no African programs that specifically focused on emotional issues of immigrant and refugee women? Again I am reminded of Osteen who further contends:

> ...go somewhere where you can dream. It may be in a church; it may be along the banks of a stream or at the park. Find someplace where your faith will be elevated. Get into an atmosphere where people build you up rather than tear you down. Find a place where people will encourage you and challenge you to be the best you can be. Spend time with people who inspire you to reach for new heights. If you associate with successful people, before long, their enthusiasm will be contagious and you will catch that vision. If you stay in an atmosphere of victory, you will develop a winning mind-set. If you hang around people of faith, your own faith will increase. It's time for you to soar with the eagles rather than pecking around with the chickens. Even when circumstances don't go your way, keep your mindset in the right direction (Ibid ps. 27-8).

Yes, it is true, but until one realizes that sitting down and thinking about one's situation will not bring any solutions to one's problem, one may find oneself in a vicious cycle of a mental trauma or mental break down. That is why it is important when people come to a new environment to find a strong support network that will guide them in their integration. In many cases, loneliness comes along with a host of negative emotions. It is however important to learn how to deal seriously with the feelings of this danger of loneliness. It is so painful that it may even bring feelings of rejection and bitterness towards the very people that you love, and then frustrations with the system that you felt would be of help. Each of these feelings has serious consequences to one's mental health. African immigrant and refugee families' experiences of isolation and helplessness produce new insights from voices that are seldom heard (Creese & Kambere, 2003).

The assumption is that African families' isolation relate to the absence of support networks and the demands and social organization of their work that reduce their possibilities to maintain meaningful social relations. Feelings of guilt and shame are likely to surface as a result, thus leading to further isolation from even your very best friends or family members that could be of help. In a research done on African immigrant and refugee women (2004), the following was identified:

> All my days in the first place was crying with nobody to comfort me, I felt isolated and abandoned, disappointed that there was no help from my small community. I didn't know about any services that help African community, they didn't tell me anything where to reach some other people. I tried to ask where maybe I could reach my own people who could understand me, but I didn't have any... I was living in a community with other ethnic groups, but they didn't really come to help me. I didn't really know anybody; that is really depressing and all my time was crying, trying to comfort myself (Kambere, focus group: p. 36).

I recall having feelings of wanting to go back to my former country, a place that I had run from for safety. I felt that life would be much better if I went back and died there than staying in a place where I was terribly isolated and with no support network. I chose to depend on my landlord's wife for a support network. I recall one time she took me to a community clinic near where we lived. She had informed me that at the clinic, they have nurses who usually visit isolated women like me and sometimes take them out for parent-child play circles. I had no idea what she was talking about, but I decided to follow her lead.

After she had introduced me to the clinic staff that she knew, she talked with the in-take worker. From this introduction, I now know who the person was, and she took all details about me. One week later, a community nurse came to visit me and found me very lonely in my house-very depressed and frustrated. As mentioned earlier, she asked me questions that I dreaded to hear. At the time, my four boys were very little. She found them playing around in the house, climbing on the chairs and making lots of noise, noise which was added stress on me. I wanted my quiet time and my own space!

My sons needed attention, which I was not aware they lacked because of my own turmoil. The nurse's visit to me was felt by one of my sons as taking my attention from him, thus taking matters even further by interrupting me from focusing on the guest that was around. I resorted to what I was familiar with from my cultural upbringing. I got the kid spanked in the presence of the nurse. The nurse who was not familiar with what I was going through or the cultural background of how we discipline kids almost collapsed on the chair. Her eyes turning red, as a reaction to something considered abusive in her Canadian upbringing. We were coming from two cultural backgrounds where we could not understand each other's way of child upbringing.

As a professional, I have learnt from the nurse's reaction the importance of cultural competence or understanding before venturing to help someone coming from a culture other than yours. She came to a new immigrant woman's family with no prior knowledge about how things are done in my culture. I was not informed either about the magnitude of spanking a child, let alone in front of the professional, but the psychological impact this might cause on the child who needed attention from a mother! The nurse's reaction and my own were both conflicting cultural misunderstandings which I feel was a failure on this professional's part.

First of all, being a community nurse as she had introduced herself, she should have identified some of the symptoms of depression that I was experiencing at the time. She found me in the house on a very hot day, simply sleeping on the couch not even outside at the park to play with my children. Couldn't she have figured out that I was under some kind of depression, especially when she talked and I never responded to her questions? There are bountiful signs and symptoms that help a healthcare professional to determine if a person is suffering from depression, symptoms that must represent a change from the way the person used to function.

Yes, she had no prior knowledge about my previous functioning. In my case, at least one of the symptoms I presented was lack of interest in her discussion, and loss of interest or pleasure in outside activities, which I presented as she came in my house. Which woman could simply lock the children in the house on a hot day without taking them out to the park?

Couldn't she have offered to take us to the park where the children could play while she developed a rapport with me?

After her shock, she explained later how it was against the law in Canada to spank children. Who could have informed me when I was simply locked in my own emotions? She could have done her research about how immigrant women's adjusting to a new culture can lead to a whole lot of changes in their life and consequently, create stress and a sense of loss of control. Some of the things she started explaining to me did not make any sense to me whatsoever. I started questioning whether she knew what she was talking about until a few months later when a social worker from the Ministry of children and family development appeared at our door wanting to apprehend our children alleging that we had left the children alone in the house; as I have mentioned earlier.

This was an added torture to me because, I was not used to this consistent monitoring of my private affairs. We were put in such a panic that we never wanted to trust these ministry people who we felt were only intruders into our personal life. The ministry person or child protection person had phoned our house and one of my sons, picked the phone and started answering questions as he was asked. The person wanted to talk to my husband regarding our financial assistance.

It had nothing to do with child neglect or anything. When the worker wanted to talk to my husband who was outside washing the car, the little boy said, "He was not around." Within minutes, someone was at the door to come and take the children away. This created more panic for me personally because I had started taking classes for my general education, only to be called by my instructors that I had left my children alone at home. I could not understand why we were being followed up by the very system that I felt was there to protect us.

Evidently the feelings of isolation manifested themselves in my life in many aspects of life. As I work with many immigrant and refugee women, I have heard countless stories how these families who arrive in the greater Vancouver Region, British Columbia continue to face difficulties with the challenges of adjusting to life here in their new home. In addition to being victims of traumatic experiences, many of them struggle to deal with tasks such as learning a new language, adjusting to a new culture, ascertaining the availability of services and struggling with the social systems which sometimes do not seem to be friendly when it comes to social expectations, particularly cross-cultural parenting.

Additionally, looking for accommodation and juggling with the social demands is as traumatizing as leaving their own countries of origin. These stressors become a part of their daily existence, resulting in constant fear, anxiety, depression, sleep disturbances and headaches (Akinshulure-Smith, 2002). It is evident that women in particular are frustrated by a lack of information on how to locate particular places and the complex set of new tasks that are involved upon arrival. In another study by Kambere (2004: p.45-focus group), one woman laments about her frustration with the system:

> ...you are new in the country, you don't know how to approach people, I went back to the welfare office and told them my problem; they said, "we don't have anything to do for you"... I told them, "I am from Africa" and of course, hearing you are from Africa, you are like a continent they don't know anything about, so that really depressed me.

These comments are reflective of the disillusionment African immigrant and refugee families are faced with as they integrate in their new society. Many of them struggle to deal with issues, such as a lack of support network, information, resources and the confusion of cultural competency on the mainstream counseling and support professional side. The language barriers, unmet expectations and struggles with role reversal are all triggers of anxiety, depression, headaches and loss of self-esteem, which consequently are all symptoms of trauma, leading to mental health problems in this population. The findings in the above studies demonstrate, that African immigrant and refugee families coming from war torn countries are further re-traumatized by post-migration experiences, particularly the lack of holistic and culturally competent services, which affect their integration process (Masinda & Kambere, 2008).

The result of lacking comprehensive services is that the African population tends to blame settlement workers and mainstream professionals for not being able to deliver appropriate services to them instead of understanding these deficiencies result from the institutional environment. In some aspects, services offered by agencies are not equipped to address the demands of African immigrant and refugee families on a holistic level (Calliste et al., 2000; Masinda & Kambere, 2008). There are many positive benefits that governments and societies have left dormant in the lives of these individuals that could be revived to benefit other people. Having been a professional in the very system that I felt was traumatizing me, I have the understanding of the effects of cultural understanding before coming to any conclusion about people that have had prior traumatic experiences.

I came to a new country with expectations of getting immediate help with a horde of pains that I was carrying. I did not expect a society where a professional would almost collapse in my living room when she saw how I tried to discipline my child. Some of these experiences that I have highlighted in this chapter could be an obstacle to professionals reaching a hurting population. As well, lack of knowledge about the culture that professionals work with could also lead to the isolation of the very people that would benefit from the mainstream help.

When these individuals lose trust in mainstream professionals, they resort to isolation from everyone who could be of help and this leads to some mental health problems. When these women have had so many disappointments, they end up shutting their doors to professionals. Their expectations of the new society are totally different from what they find, especially in regards to housing, parenting and the insecurity feeling caused by the new system. All these instead add more stress to the already 'wounded' immigrants. All these conditions have profound impact on the integration process of refugee and immigrant women. Subsequently, these identified situations need to be fully understood by the policy makers, and agencies providing settlement services to these individual groups.

Create organizational and professional's competence

My intention of writing this section is not to produce an academic paper, but to try to highlight a few points of concern as professionals begin to deal with Sub-Saharan AIR women. George W. Doherty (1999) points out:

> Counselors should have knowledge of the culture they work in as part of their expertise and competence...the experience of the counselor [is vital]. A cultural group or the information on it in the relevant professional literature serves as a source of hypotheses, to be verified, discarded and/or modified based on acquisition of further information. Working together with

counselors from the culture could vastly improve the probability of success in appropriate interventions.

Women may not find the services offered to them helpful because of the lack of understanding of the experiences these women go through pre-migration. One woman states:

...health and social service professionals continue to lack understanding of the complex circumstances of refugee women. Professionals showed little interest in learning about what had happened to [us, but only we are] given antidepressant medication (quoted by Berman, Rosa & Marroquin, 2006, p.46).

From African immigrant women's perspectives, professionals need to have an approach of working with them relevant to their suffering from both clinical and anthropological perspectives. This would help professionals to widen their understanding of traumatized women's experiences. Such an approach would give the professionals some knowledge that is distinct from the deeply entrenched Western based scientific models, which, to the women, is often unable to provide them concrete understanding of the needs and concerns that they have.

As we continue to see a growing numbers of refugee and immigrants arrive in Canada from troubled war-torn countries, the challenge for professionals, such as social workers and mental health workers dealing with these immigrants, is to ensure that they are culturally competent and aware of the issues these people come with. In my professional practice with different ethnic groups, I have had the opportunity to be informed that cultural competency is very vital while working with clients from ethno-cultural groups other than mine. The cultural knowledge of the rituals, social supports, customs and habits can help in treating people who have had past negative experiences. To demonstrate the central role of cultural competence, Dutton (1998) notes that some cultures have

Social norms that value the family as the center of help-seeking or that hold the integrity for the family as a higher value than the welfare of an individual within it. It is important for trauma clinicians to recognize and appreciate the meaning of help-seeking for traumatized persons among different cultural groups (p.1).

Most importantly, multicultural settlement workers and social workers have to do their best to create conditions for maximizing their ability to understand the functioning of clients, their points of strength and areas in which they may be suffering or need assistance. On the other hand, social workers and many other mental health professionals must be aware of the secondary re-traumatization and burnout in working with traumatized clients. It is also important to ascertain the individual's spiritual roots and encourage them to use the church family as a way of reconnecting and healing from the loss or any memories that they might have had. For instance, Tankink's (2007) observation when she participated in the born-again churches in Mbarara District, Southwestern Uganda suggests that when victims of war turn to their faith, they find healing from the support of the pastor's message about confronting past memories.

She demonstrates some of her findings as she attended a born again faith church and the variety of definitions she identified from people who had suffered war trauma.

She identifies that:

...the pastor teaches the people how to place those memories as an almost tangible object outside themselves. He uses a kind of self-control, characterized by a mental stop and followed by a mental concentration on God. By doing this, one can release oneself from the painful memories, inducing feelings of relief and relaxation (p.212).

Some of this information might be uncommon in some of the approaches that professionals in the Western treatment or counseling model take because talking about such things in the West is considered a private, and personal matter.

It is therefore important for professionals to be informed about some of the approaches that have been used in other cultures when dealing with victims of war or any kind of loss. To the AIR women, prayer is not out of context when communities have been faced with calamity. For immigrants and refugees, help-seeking behaviors and treatment expectations are often different than for other groups. Social workers and professionals dealing with these groups need to help the client negotiate conflicting cultural demands as they deal with change (Dutton, 1998 and Tankink, 2007). It is also important for professionals working with immigrant and refugee clients with symptoms of PTSD to recognize that assessment may be extremely complicated because of the difficulty of establishing trust, especially where the methods that they are familiar with in their countries of origin, such as healing of loss, are not going to be utilized. Further, they may become reluctant to talk about traumatic events that can reactivate past memories (Allen, 2001).

In working with this population, tremendous efforts are needed to identify pre-migration stressors and how such stressors could be dealt with in their own cultural healing. It is also important for psychiatrists, psychologists, social workers, nurses, counselors, clergy and others with an interest in the treatment of this population to offer people alternative ways to think, feel and experience by linking everything with God (Tankink, 2007), especially working with ethnic groups whose strong belief is in a high power.

Another woman suggests the following:

Some of us AIR Women, we had pre-immigration stress due to war in addition to the stress of migration. We need information that can raise awareness of the issues of mental illness and its treatments. We are sometimes in denial that we have some emotional trauma, and we need ethno-specific workers who can support and listen to us (focus group # 3, 2008).

In my own experience working and interacting with this population, it is therefore important to be aware of the list of symptoms which constitute PTSD as these are usually presented by many people who have suffered traumatic experiences. What may be helpful is the realization that there are aspects of pain and distressing experiences that have to be related to and understood by clinicians as well as mental health professionals.

After you have heard from them, this will help you make an informed judgment, let it be in schools, hospitals or at work. Tackling the complex mental health needs of refugees is particularly challenging for both primary care providers and mental health professionals. There is a debate on the applicability of PTSD to immigrants and refugees, yet their experiences have not been supported and authenticated (Freidman & Jaranson, 1994).

Women further elaborate on their expectations from professionals that they assume have the solutions to their problems. Consider the following script:

> The life we are living is not life we expected. They put companies to help us. You go there to tell your problems to a counselor, they listen, and then the only thing they tell you is that we will get back to you and they never get back forever. This causes stress; professionals add more stress to the refugees" (Focus group # 3, 2008).
>
> The participants in this study complained that due to the pain of trying to integrate while familiarizing themselves with the new system, they could not function without any medication to relieve their stress. Additionally, even the medication that they received was only temporary; it did not take away the pain. Loice explains: We never knew what stress is until we got here. You become useless to yourself. You have constant headaches. I have developed a tendency to forget even simple appointments due to stress. I have been so restless, pain in my whole body. Sometimes I go to the kitchen, but find myself in the bathroom. So these problems have been so prevalent of our lives. We are given medicine, which temporarily controls the problems so that I can forget myself, preferring to death. Think that maybe if someone died, I would not be going through this entire trauma, [where I feel] very stressed and forgetful. Problems like these, we do not know how we are going to overcome them. Like me, due to much stress I cannot go to sleep without taking sleep aid medicine of which I sometime take more than prescribed so that they can work. But I end up oversleeping and my kids get worried. One day my children even called an ambulance after I failed to wake up. I took 6 sleeping pills!! (Focus group #3, 2008).

What professionals need to identify are the delayed and missed bereavement among these women (Boehnlein, 1987). The obvious losses that are commonly expressed include the deaths and separations encountered during flight. Exploring the individual potential traumas will eventually give professionals a broader perspective of women's strengths, a deeper understanding of what barriers and baggage they come with, either at work or in seeking for social support.

Involve ethnic communities in services planning

Improving services and outcomes for AIR women and other ethno-cultural groups is becoming a challenge for service planning especially in their mental health systems of Canadian society. Service planning has to be geared towards the situations and needs. It is my humble submission that after listening to so many stories in this narrative and my own experience, that all services will need to be capable of offering equitable care to Canada's diverse population (Chow, Law, Andermann et al., 2010) and honor the importance of place (Mensah, & Williams, 2014).

Some suggestions have been offered by women for the following to be implemented:

- Better co-ordination of policy, knowledge, and accountability
- The involvement of communities, families, and people with lived experience
- More appropriate and improved services which are culturally relevant to AIR women's needs and close to their neighborhood.

With better coordination of policy, knowledge and accountability there is recognition of the need for specific articulated plans to improve the services for Sub-Saharan African Immigrant and Refugee women. If these are coordinated at the various levels of municipalities and across different organizations and institutions then they will be more effective to meet the needs of this population. As women have narrated, the best approach would be to bring many of these actions together that would be developed around community-based and flexible services.

Such an approach would focus on policy improvement and public health interventions aimed at health promotion and illness prevention as well as interventions targeted at service improvement, which have been so restrictive for a long time. The exact extent of the plan would depend on the needs of the population and, of course, the resources available, not what the system feels the immigrants need (Kambere, 2004; Masinda & Kambere, 2008).

The involvement of communities, families and people with lived experience is vital in dealing with this population. Engaging local AIR women's groups in the planning process helps in the development of more appropriate services and also allows for linkage to community based services. The planning process will also need community engagement and knowledge exchange function that may build capacity and networks, improve awareness and access to care (Masinda & Kambere, 2008; Herman, 2003).

With a plan in place, and an engaged community, services can forge a path of collaboration and internal development. Some suggestions are outlined below in five groups of actions required to improve services for Sub-Sahara AIR populations which are related to mental health:

- Changed focus – an increased emphasis on prevention of re-traumatisation
- Improvement within services – organisational and individual cultural competence
- Improved diversity of treatment – diversity of providers, evaluation of treatment options
- Linguistic competence – improved communication plans and actions to meet Canada's diverse needs
- Needs linked to expertise – plans to offer support by people and services with expertise to areas with the AIR community so they can offer high quality care (Masinda & Kambere, 2008, 2009, 2010; Creese, 2009).

Understanding of factors that relate to clients' subjective reality based on their integration process creates trust between professional and client. The community counselor and client each have a cultural context and a set of experiences and expectations that are often widely divergent. Because of these complexities, the difficulties of adequately assessing and treating the traumatized refugee or immigrant woman may seem insurmountable if there is a lack of understanding of cultural context (Jaranson, 1991). They are working with a community that may look at treating their problems in a different context as some of the participants have outlined:

They should be asked. That is why I said, you need to understand who is this person, where they come from, it is not just for employment, you need to dig into the background. I mean it is not just digging into just because you want to spy on them for anything, but you need the roots of the issues they are dealing with and you need to know the culture where they come from, how they deal with things. Because you have to work within what they work with…Christianity, that is what helps them. You have to be able to support them through that. I mean I can imagine it is hard because a lot of Western may not practice that kind of Christianity, but if that is what helps them, the openness to discuss it and then to support the client. So the possibility for the worker to say, okay, you know, this is, I don't practice this but I can give you resources if you can't talk about it. But at least send the person where they can be helped more. You know if that is what they practice, because I think being client centered is very important, so yes. I am definitely for people to know the client, to know where they come from, what background will help them, what they like, what is it you know and also even the worker to find their intervention like. For me I know, because I practice from a Western point of view, I cannot include that kind of spiritual stuff, but I can say, I can recommend and say, please, go and pray because we are not allowed. So I hope one day there will be a place where people can actually use some kind of formal spiritual ways too. I think there are some marginal practices doing that at this point, but it is never been [officially acknowledged], if you work in a mainstream you are going to follow the mainstream thing. (Int. #1, 2008).

During our discussions, there were suggestions that women highlighted as means to help them deal with their trauma. They acknowledge that psychologists and other professionals do a good job, but do have some concerns regarding the standard way of dealing with people who have been traumatized. They understand that each culture deals with trauma differently and the standard form that is used is based on the Western way of dealing with any trauma, which they feel is not relevant to their own way of how some of them have been helped:

Let us say, the school of social work, psychology department, they have to think of other ways, dealing with immigrants cases, because in the long run, immigrants are becoming predominant population in many cities, so you can't get away with it, you know. So they need to begin thinking in a more progress way, just to get out of the box and begin thinking of how [they] train their workers in a way that they can begin looking at the population that [is] changing, the social dynamic changes in the demography, so that is one thing. Another thing is to also encourage other professionals who come from these countries if they have some practices that are not harmful and that it is commendable like the way they do with Chinese herbal medicine for example. You know why don't we study how African women in our countries or our ancestors dealt with trauma, you know, why don't we let them tell you what they did healing their trauma before they came to Canada?...whenever you bring up such question, they say oh no, no that is back ward, it is not provable, whatever [not scientifically proven]. The same thing with spirituality you know, anyone who is going to tell you, when I say, spirituality helped me, I don't even want to tell them what exactly helped me because people will not even listen, they will just say that is your own religion (laughter)...that is personal issue, yeah, they will just say that is your belief or whatever, but why don't we explore spirituality, because there are a lot of people who will tell you what really helped them. It is really my faith, whatever, so that is another thing so it would be really very interesting to explore alternative ways of supporting people, which is culturally centered, sustained or whatever.(int.#1, 2008).

Another woman has the following to say:

I also recommend that our services have programs that focus on bridging, the gap. You know when we talked about all different barriers that come through before people are ready to be employed, we need programs, we need programs, let us say like life skills programs, that is very important to teach women; we need literacy programs that are more adopted; we need program aha, we need pre-employment program that are adopted for people so during those core baggage issues that we have been talking about, it is very important... Just to understand, learning and getting to know the person and getting to know their strength and their resilience. So that is why I insist on competency, you know cultural competency, or client centered approaches or whatever. Something that prepares them to know that, yes, this person has gone through trauma, I need to understand this trauma, but only I need to understand what kind of strength this person had to deal with it (Focus group # 3, 2008).

Social gatherings and talking about their experiences are other ways African women deal with their experiences, thus bringing healing to their emotional challenges. One participant also describes how they dealt with their emotional traumas, Lisa says:

We don't have support groups in our cultures. We get together; have fun, talk about countries. We play our music. Some people who want to cry, they cry. Some people who want to talk about their childhood, they do and cry especially on special holidays, we used to make traditional things, pray. That's how we survive. (Focus group # 2, 2008).

Some of the women disclosed how they avoided continuing with counseling sessions with professionals whom they felt were not culturally trained to deal with problems related to their own African way as one woman explains her situation:

I just looked at him, like are you kidding me (laughter), I think he was trying to be helpful within the context he has been prepared to. I thought that must be hard. How can this help me, I did not even see that being helpful for me whatsoever. Eventually, I am the one who figured out myself what to do next. Because eventually I think I just started more introspection myself and just my spirituality helped me. I remember I had scheduled four sessions of counseling with him. I went to two of them and then the second one I told him, can you let me skip the two remaining and if I need you, I will let you know, but if I don't need them, I don't have to come. So I remember on the phone, I called him and said, don't worry, I have figured it out myself. (Int. #1, 2008).

Another one says:

My nurse came to visit me and I was complaining that the house was too expensive and I don't have money...and she said, what do you expect, you came from Africa, you are lucky, so be grateful! ...I never accepted her in my house again" (Interview, Jane Francis, 2009).

It may be said that professionals seeing African immigrant and refugee clients need to work within a middle ground approach between pharmacological treatment and anthropological approach. For instance, for some other cultures, the applicability of the Western model of PTSD treatment may not be of great significance. As Brady, Sonne & Roberts (1995) point out, it might be wrong to focus on the individual in cultures where symptoms and signs of trauma may have different meanings. Some may feel their trauma related symptoms may be related to lack of closure to their deceased relatives whom they never had the opportunity to participate in the cultural ceremonies. Others might have feeling that they have not fulfilled the obligations required of them according their cultural norms.

This echoes Dyregov, Gupta, Gjestad & Raundalen's (2002) assumption, that "culture can create meaningful systems that explain the causes of trauma, provide ritual and healing strategies through which one can express and heal one's reaction and at the same time reconnect with the group" (p.3).

One of the participants in this project has this to say:

Yeah, people are dealing with so many struggles with their families, you know a mum has been screened, if they know that their child is languishing in the refugee camp, you know, how do you think a mum will be working there happily if they know that their child is languishing in a refugee camp, you know? There is a lot of heartache you know, that can cause like you know a lot of emotional and psychological effects. People you know underestimate how the emotional trauma can handicap someone, you know. Because if you don't feel well, if your emotional stability is not well addressed, it is very rare for you to kind of go and perform well on the job. So I think, I should not say that you should deal with one after another because most of the time people don't have actually the luxury of dealing with that when they need the money, but it is always that these programs should be simultaneous, they should be, if you see that your clients when they come to ask for a job, that there is a lot of baggage. You have to address this baggage at the same time (Int. #.1 African counselor, 2008).

SECTION V

LAST THOUGHTS

In narrating my own story and hearing other women's narratives, I felt the healing from my own past. I realize that sharing these women's testimonies was a journey that needed another person to be around and be supportive in their walk through the difficult voyage of the unknown. When I started writing my own narrative, I did not have an understanding that sharing and putting my own story in print would also allow more healing on my part, especially when I felt as though I was talking to a trusted person, i.e. the paper which could listen and not judge me. I felt given the opportunity to tell my experience from childhood to adulthood as a backbone to my healing and progressively looking at things in a more positive manner.

I have come to realize that writing this book was not only for you to hear my story, but also for myself to get the healing that only I, the writer was able to demonstrate in my own words. I have found this book very healing in my journey through life's circumstances. I would like to share a short story here about the dangers of not dealing with our past traumas before we are able to move on with our lives in a new environment. In 2007, I found myself hit by a past trauma I should have dealt with previously! It hit me so hard that it pained me more than it did over 25 years ago.

I thought I had dealt with it, but to my surprise, it simply resurfaced as if it had just happened that very day. I cried, had feelings of regrets, betrayal and disappointment more than I did then; but no remedial mechanism helped me whatsoever. Why am I talking about it now? I simply came to realize that we immigrant women come from cultures where we are culturally trained to simply bury our pains and move on with life because some of these circumstances are considered normal for women.

What I need to share with women immigrants and any other women that come from a familiar culture such as mine, is that it is not wise to keep your trauma without dealing with it as you start a new life. It will eventually come to hit you in a way that might even paralyze you! When I found myself in this storm, I looked for people outside my sphere of influence that could sympathize with me and say, "Sorry Edith, it will be okay, you will be fine", but I found no help whatsoever.

In the midst of that, I resorted to reading any books that I found that had been written by women. I knew they had a story that they had to share, which would bring solace to me, which I will say, some of them helped as I read their personal stories. So my point and advice to my audience is, start reading something if you are able to. You will find that you are not alone in your journey. You will find other people who have had similar or worse situations than yours. This way, you will begin to develop a positive attitude about your situation and about yourself.

I understand some of the lifestyle of new immigrants to a new society. Self-care is not a priority, especially when they are faced with a host of demands as they try to integrate. When we come to a new society, the first thing we think of is survival of the fittest, economic hardships and demands, which finally distract us from the essentials of health care.

We easily forget that we came wounded and need to heal or get some cleaning up of our past mess/trauma before we can be able to function well in a new environment. You cannot be functional in any environment when you still have a crushed, wounded spirit that needs to be cleaned. Band aids do not help heal past traumas. Anything that scratches the wound will make it bleed to the point that you may not be able to have the energy to walk! Let your past-trauma first be cleaned so that you become functional in your new home. I have come to realize through my personal experience that even the slightest reminder or trigger of your past trauma will paralyze you to the point that you may not be able to function well under the heat of life circumstances in your new society.

To be honest with my audience, I had little regard for writing huge papers, but I had to do something, write my story! As I started writing, I found that I was talking to myself and the paper and pen were my audience that did not want to judge me by my looks, the way I talk, or the color of my accent, but only to listen and give me the opportunity to talk. I felt someone was listening and lifting me up. I know most of us do not have the luxury of reading and writing when we are faced with challenges of life's demands.

To the best of my knowledge, do not despair, and stop blaming yourself thinking that it is too late to be reading a book. Alternatively, seek professional help that you feel you trust before it is too late. In most cases, we are so busy working and taking care of families, teenage sons and daughters who are driving us crazy due to cross-cultural parenting;

and looking after young adults as I am currently doing, trying to be a good house wife, running home errands and to some of you helping people who need your support. Please, get started and do something for yourself, you will not regret it. Trying to make everyone happy but don't neglect and forget the most important thing: self-care. Do not forget to seek professional help from someone who cares about your well-being; it is the worst thing that you can do to yourself!

During my 2007 crisis, I sought help from my faith sisters, friends who consistently supported me and assured me that healing will for sure come and the past trauma will be no more, an issue to hold me a slave or in bondage. Memories will still be there, but they will not be as painful if you have exposed the trauma and shared it with those who will hold your hand and say, "Tomorrow will look different than today."

I have come to realize the accomplishments and strength that I have achieved as I have walked this journey that has not only been strenuous, but also traumatic. My journey and that of the women in this context have had experiences that only a listening ear would be proud of what we each have accomplished in our own ways and what we have shared as a result. We cannot call ourselves failures, but survivors who have walked the odds of circumstances not of our own making. Our narratives have been a journey of narrative exposure therapy based on our own way of testimony therapy, which has helped us in understanding that the system that is there to help us in our integration process needs to hear what we need when we come to meet mainstream trained professionals.

The stories that have been shared in this book have highlighted the need to recognize torture in African refugee women, whose stories might have shed light on the indicators of posttraumatic stress in torture survivors, and provide additional resources to care for them as they integrate. In my own voyage of hills and mountains, I have come to realize the concept of "not giving up on your dream no matter how old you may think you are." What you need is encouragement from someone who has had similar experiences or someone who has a sympathetic heart to guide you in your walk, someone to tell you that you will succeed no matter the odds. In this way, you will find the hope that you need; if you can only keep your head up right with a positive attitude.

What do I mean by hope? Joyce Meyer (July, Enjoying every day Magazine, 2008) talks about how hope is something favorable that we are confidently expecting. "It's looking forward with anticipation of something good. Hope is what keeps us from giving up during hard times" (p.1). It is important for many of you readers to not allow hard times to keep you from looking forward to what you have hoped for all these years of your struggles. Refuse to give up hope. Start expecting for something good and you will surely get it. To this day, it is hope that still keeps me from giving up in tough times of parenting my four adult boys.

I know, as women, we all go through tough times, especially the immigrant women who come with high expectations of fulfilling their aspirations, and when tough times come, you start wondering whether things will ever change. That is what hope is all about (Meyer, 2008). It is only to maintain a positive attitude of expecting good things to happen which enable you to maintain a sane mind. It costs you nothing to maintain hope, but it may cost you a whole lot to lose it!

In writing about my traumatic experience and that of the women, it was my ambition to integrate their stories and their wisdom of how they dealt with their emotions, as well as some of the African counselors who had borne witness to the psychological effects of war and to set forth in a unique comparison of stories that needed to be told (Judith, 1997).

As I was writing these narratives, I knew I was sharing with women who have lived with their past pains. Each time such memories interfere with your daily work, you have always told yourself that the pain is an illusion, that it is not true, thinking that the next day, will bring a new hope and new music for you to dance to. I believe there are many untold stories such as these women have lived with. I only hope that as we have shared our stories, some of the readers will be encouraged to stand firm and know that they are not alone.

I am aware of women that have had their aspirations and dreams shattered due to the pains that they experienced and the future does not appear to have any glimpse of happiness. I say to them, be assured that as long as you still have breath, don't rule anything out. I want to tell you that you don't need to live controlled by these very pains that were inflicted on you by someone else. As you accept to live in the past, the very person continues to hold you hostage even when you are on the road to recovery or living on the other side of the ocean. Lamenting about them is what makes it even more painful and giving power to the situation. You don't want to be a slave of the very things that have caused your life long pains and bitter memories.

As you read the stories of these women, I believe there are many untold stories such as these women shared because you have not had someone to motivate you do so. Some of you have lived with stories and wounds of rape, disappointment and rejections that you cannot share with anyone, except you and your heart. The two beings are the only ones that know the pain, not even your mother, your daughter, and to some of us, our beloved husbands! I hope as you have heard and read our narratives, you will be encouraged to stand firm and know that you have many sisters behind you who have had their own share that was not of their own making.

Some women have become slaves of shame like I was; I want to tell you that you don't need to live in the pit of shame. Believe that no matter what the situation has been or what is going on in your life, remain hopeful and know that your situation is shared by many women reading this script as well as those who have shared their stories. Your situation can change because it is not engraved in stone, although the scars do not have any solution, unfortunately. I know what it means by leaving in the past; the past is so painful that you do not want to even look back.

I encourage many of you who are reading these narratives, whether men, girls and children who have had their own shares of trauma as a result of some past pains- quit receiving all the accusations; quit allowing the condemning voices to take root, crowding out the good things of your life (Osteen, 2005). Make your past pains as a stepping stool to build your self-esteem. To assure you, living in the past is the worst ever experience that one would dread to live. There is no pain as that of living in the past, especially if your past was dreadful! Most of you were thrown in pits that were not of your own choosing, someone else threw you there, be it the political situation in your country or the person that raped you; vengeance is not yours, but God's.

Realizing that whoever threw you in the pit does not even know how much it hurt you! No matter how much you screamed into their eyes about the pain they caused you or how much it hurt you, they would not get it. Unfortunately they don't even have a clue how much it affected your life, relationship with your husband, your children, even your associates! Simply forgive them not only for their destructive actions, but also for their ignorance. My dear reader, you have no choice, if you want to get out of the pit! (Moore, 2007).

As we move on reading and pouring our hearts of hurts to each other, we will find strength from other women's narratives. Each of us had dreams and those dreams are still alive; they need to be produced to bear fruits that may help others who have gone through our experiences.

It is never too late to re-kindle your dreams. Many of you might have struggled in your academic aspirations as I did.

I want to tell you that it is never too late until you are out of breath. My life story about my struggle with school, especially with mathematics was dreadful. For some of you reading this book, women who have shared in this narrative are your sisters who share with you and encourage you to keep up the torch. There are people behind you who would love to read your story of hope and aspirations as these women have shared. I wish I had the opportunity to read words shared by bestselling authors such as Osteen (2005), whose words are inspirational. He advises, "When you go through failures and disappointments, don't sit around in self-pity. Don't go month after month condemning yourself and rejecting yourself" (p.92). Be encouraged by these women's stories and at the end of the tunnel, you will see light.

Everyone has their own way of dealing with their own fears and how these fears have become a stepping stone to be able to face life's challenges, with hope and courage. I believe everyone has a story to share, but have not had the motivation or the force behind them to be able to share with other people like them. When I was faced with these failures, the only hope I still had were people who believed in me, my family members. When my employers and colleagues at work judged me by the color of my accent, I found hope in my friends who believed in me and encouraged me to take a different step forward.

So, what I want to share with you in these concluding remarks is for you readers to continue on with your hopes; it is never too late. I could not understand that I would be able to graduate with a Masters degree and be able to write what you are reading now. It is a matter of connecting with the right people who will believe in you; I had those people when I almost gave up on my desires.

In our sharing, even though some of the women came to Canada carrying this baggage of shame where they were not able to share such traumatic experiences with their family members in fear of being labeled as outcasts, our connection was an open space to get the support that there were people who cared. The fear to talk about such incidents because if they did, they might lose whatever support they had in the community was no longer an issue as some women narrated. They experienced some sort of resilience when they found support from their family members who encouraged them to not listen to criticisms of being ostracized by their husband about the rape and humiliation.

It is demonstrated in the women's stories how in many instances they feared that they would not be believed or would be blamed by the relatives of the perpetrators if they revealed to them what happened. When such secrets are hidden with no formal counseling or having a support network in the refugee camps where these incidents happened, and when you who are professionals meet these women in their offices, you are seeing a person whose outward look is only masking pain coupled with family disruption. Additionally, you are meeting a woman who is unable to articulate herself in the Canadian English, the official language of the country, who has also been judged by employers about her local English accent. These emotions may cause a woman to experience a sense of personal disarray, emotional trauma, and imposed isolation thus leading to a lack of a social support network.

When they are faced with these emotions, it is vital through their narrative for professionals to allow them to exercise what they are familiar with, prayer, which is a tool, in which they usually find strength. Mullica (2007) has given light about how trauma victims have answers to their problems, especially if they are given space to talk among themselves as victims about their situations. Evidently, there is joy as I saw in these women sharing their personal stories, as I also shared mine, which rekindled new hope for a brighter future. Sharing personal stories helped all of us to open up about what some of the women had harbored for years.

We all felt that we were resilient women who were able to survive our ordeals without any formal counseling. From the women's sharing, there was strength that was evident as friendships and a support network were established. There was a sense of hope even though some of them still had a sense of emptiness and insecurity that they could not take away instantly due to the long silence of not having had someone who shared similar experiences as theirs.

What these women were used to before they got resettled into Canada is the therapy they got from gatherings that were usually informal. They met either when they were fetching water or firewood, experiences which are remote in their new society. When there were issues such as family abuse, marital problems, the therapy they got was either through an extended family support network or through women's social gatherings and in many cases on an adhoc basis. During such socialization moments, they would talk about some of their family problems in an "informal setting" which in most cases is labeled as "gossip." But to these women, these kinds of arrangements helped them a great deal. Women who found themselves in such a traumatic situations would learn that their next neighbors were also faced with similar issues.

Consequently, a support network evolved through such gossip where women would not feel alone or isolated. A woman would find empowerment through other women's stories. Evidently, in Canada, the only opportunity women find is if there is a group of women participants involved in some discussion such as in this script for this narrative.

When these Sub Saharan AIR women come to a new society, such as Canada, they find a different approach to life. They find an approach where they have to make appointments after appointments. In most cases, it may take a week before they hear back from the professionals they want to meet. Structured programs and meeting with people who are not familiar with the ways of dealing with their trauma like in their countries of origin, or cultures which are totally different from their own is an aspect that they have to deal with. Developing trust with such professionals becomes very difficult, if not impossible, as you have heard from the women's narratives.

The general feeling that all the participants had was that, instead of professionals together with these women mutually coming up with a plan of action on how their health should be treated and/or services should be provided to them, professionals assume the role of being "experts" and decide on what is in the best interest for the very people who feel they know what they need. They have highlighted the importance of a holistic approach; without it they become reluctant to access services relevant to their needs.

I have also had the opportunity to learn from the participants who feel that the society to which they came to live does not understand or know enough about the psychological effects of war trauma and the emotional change this brings to them. Most of them have identified how they do not want to seek treatment due to lack of knowledge by professionals on how they dealt with mental illness or trauma in their own cultures. Besides, no one of these women would feel comfortable discussing anything to do with psychiatric illness because that is not how the mental health or psychiatric is called in their cultures.

It is important for organizations that serve victims of war to learn about the local idioms of distress or trauma and how psychologically it is experienced, expressed, and understood in the diverse African specific cultural contexts. As a professional myself, we still have a long road ahead of us to understand culturally specific patterns of help-seeking behavior. There is still need to learn traditional ways of coping with trauma or emotional distress in order to be able to identify locally available resources within these participants' communities that can promote healing and adaptation. One participant had this to say:

> I think social workers don't even ask you how you are doing (Ophelia), while the other one laments: I think it is those welfare people that should link you with the people who should support you. I think so (Comfort). I think counselors, counselors at welcome house…they should connect the newcomers to different [support services and our African ethnic community members] because newcomers are leaving from various countries, coming to Canada, okay, they are coming to Canada to be welcomed the way [we are supposed to be treated] (Josephine). Another woman laments, for example I have a social worker who is from …, my goodness (with raised voice and anger in the client's expression), every question I asked, there is no answer I have to look for answers on my own…yes, I told him this is it this is the way you will be working with me… you are so smart (she slams her hands together in rage and a sound from her hand shake explodes out) and like these things don't work the way I expected, it is your job, you have been paid to do this (Onilia) (Kambere, 2004: focus group).

I have found in our own experiences and my professional work with this group of women who have had past trauma, that trust and expectation is prevalent. Some of them criticize professionals who have good intentions of helping out, but it is the mechanism with which to deal with their emotional baggage that needs to be addressed in a more cross-cultural approach.

Even though I am an insider/outsider in this exercise, as a professional, I have found strength hearing people with similar experiences share their coping mechanisms with their past. This change in thinking has also brought growth and change in attitude and the way I perceive the world that sometimes is not friendly to all who live in it. This change of perception has brought patience-understanding of how the world social connection could influence one's perception about other people around them, especially the people we serve.

I am mindful of how we are always affected by our past if we do not find people who share with us what the past was like and how they were able to deal with it. Each of our experiences were painful and we all question why they ever happened. Though painful and negative the experiences might have been, we all have found strength to be able to support one another. Especially when I shared my own disappointment with the systems in every society where I have lived, I hear other women comment on how they have been encouraged and strengthened by my own stories of pain.

I have placed the AIR women's stories and my story at the center of my study. The motivation behind sharing our stories in this script as a professional and immigrant woman who went through my own challenges, and the re-traumatization as I tried to integrate into the Canadian system are all factors that I believe will bring healing to some of those who are reading this book, with an understanding that other women have been there in your pit! In my own sharing with the women during our interaction, we did not see ourselves as affected women or as helpless victims, but rather as a reminder of our greater inner strength to live.

Every one of these women in this book has this potential, which can serve as a resource, and as a source of overcoming extreme situations. It is important to discover these sources in the course of therapy and to put them to good use in further shaping these women's lives. Furthermore, it is important to discover the potential within the women's stories, in meeting with other affected women, who are jointly working on a new basis for their lives and who find a great number of resources within their cultural identity. Even as I have shared my own experiences of pain and hearing that of the other women, I have realized that it is not good to remain in one's pain, but to give oneself a goal and work on it. As you work on your goal, it will lead you to your aspiration. Within you, find self-motivation to get you out of the closet.

It is also important to be courageous to speak up and not shy away to speak when you are put down. This will lead you to bottling up issues that might surface at a later time resulting in self-destruction or an angry outburst. It may finally put you into a panic mood where you will not be able to function well to your ability because you are always fearful of what is going to be spoken to you. Refuse the lies of condemnation or being put down. We may have the genetic make up for leadership or determination, but also environmental factors are factors that may be a pull or push factor to self-diminishing. If these women get mentors to hold their hands, it will lead them to a different perspective of seeing and doing things as you have read in the script.

In my own experience of being judged by my accent, I thankfully found some strength through friends who believed in me. I was told to start work in an only African organization, because that is where some people who did not know me well felt I was suitable to work. Initially, it was painful; but thankfully my husband and I had to start an African organization, Umoja Operation Compassion, which serves African immigrant and refugee families that come from war trauma countries.

As I write this book, I am excited that this organization has extended its services to many immigrants and refugees from all troubled war countries. Such an achievement to reach out to other immigrants from different nationalities gives me joy, strength and a sense of the real "woman of status!" Out of this organization, women have shared their personal stories with me as I share with them while motivating them how it is possible that we can get out of our pits with triumph and victorious. Such information becomes realistic because they share while sitting under the roof of an organization started by the very woman who went through similar experiences as theirs.

At this organization, I have had the joy and privilege of sharing my own personal story of trauma. I have also had the opportunity of hearing women describe horrific accounts of abuse and trauma in the countries they fled. I am informed of the difficulties they are facing in their integration process into the Canadian society. Through our social interaction at this organization, women have described the difficulties of their experiences of integrating successfully into Canadian society because it is very difficult to find good jobs that utilize their prior training and education.

As we all sat together reminiscing our pains and triumphs, we saw ourselves as culturally deprived in the new environment. Through our ordeals, we felt a sense of victory with an understanding that we have come a long way and have the resources that no one will take from us, our strength! When professionals try to help us as we settle in our new environment, we need those professionals who will identify these resources that we come with. Our resources are within us, which clinicians and professionals might integrate into the treatment model.

It is also important that we are given the hope and structure of how to go about the new systems that sometimes become an added trauma to the already traumatized AIR woman. One friend of mine who had read and heard much of my personal story sent me this encouraging word, stating that we as immigrants are already prize winners, looking at the battles that we have already won, the long voyage to Canada, the confinement in refugee camps and surviving the ordeal of rapes and separations from our families. She said, "Edith, you are a prize winner by virtue of your story that has touched me, which I believe will also touch millions of other women who will read your book".

Even though I have shared my own personal story and my experience of working with my fellow AIR women, this experience has not been without its own trauma. In doing the AIR women's narratives I wanted to bring a clear picture to the readers about our struggles and how, through a positive attitude and the helping hand that we found along the way, we were able to pass through our life huddles. The women in this script together with my own experience respond to what scholars and professionals alike know which usually gets left out when the experiences of such a group is translated in the language of the status quo.

This study reacts to common omission of African voices, as well as to the bias, misconception and misrepresentation that commonly color the mainstream narratives of Africans and their experiences. The AIR women's stories are therefore, a way of challenging the status quo and reclaiming the public space of production of knowledge in favor of the marginalized, in that it seeks to provide an avenue for authentic marginalized African voices to describe their experience in their own words and their own way.

My own struggles and those of other African refugee women in my community have inspired me to document our stories. On my own refugee journey, I have come to experience how hard it is to rebuild one's life and move forward within an everyday climate of discrimination and marginalization. I know though the fact that I am an educated woman who has made my path easy. It has given me more power to access resources. My situation is in no way comparable to, for example, the despair of a mother of two who can't speak English and whose welfare cheque has been cut.

How do such African refugee women survive in an alien world that deprives them of the most basic needs? And yet they do, through their amazing spirit of resilience, resourcefulness and determination. I have witnessed and realized that many of the women are truly heroines in our midst, but the kind that live in the shadow of marginality. This project was born out of my desire to record their struggles and victories as a way of giving them the recognition they so deserve. As I end this book, I would like to pay tribute to one of the women, a very long time councilor in the African community who was tragically murdered by the very woman she was trying to help, who was troubled by mental health illness. This work is dedicated to her services to the African community.

One great outcome of this project was that because of sharing our personal and intimate stories, my friendship with all the women deepened. I experienced a stronger feeling of empathy, connection and support, and I hope this was a mutual feeling. I must acknowledge that I benefited the most from this project, not just that I was able to work through my narrative, but also because I learned tremendous insight and wisdom from interacting with these women.

CONCLUSION

My book has come to the end. In writing this book my main goal has been to contribute to the healing process and provide a voice for many silent immigrant and refugee women living with trauma.

This book is full of women's stories. The women's stories exemplify both trauma and people's willingness to help other individuals. The book narrates stories of resilience as one of the most important features of being human, finding the strength needed to overcome the problems we face.

As I finish writing this book, a great deal of my healing has already taken place. Writing this book helped me to bring light and joy to the silent spaces of pain that remained from my journey into exile and migration to Canada.

Writing this book has also magnified my identity as a proud Ugandan and Canadian. My Ugandan identity is planted in my childhood, embedded in family love and challenges with education, and also the political violence that annulled hopes and wounded hearts. My life of exile was filled with the discoveries of unbelievably caring people, and my life was made richer for it. My Canadian identity is rooted in finding a new home, and fuelling my soul with caring, support and understanding from my fellow Canadians alongside the challenges associated with some seeing me as a 'foreigner' who does not belong here. With my Canadian identity I have come to be part of a larger mosaic culture characterized by fairness, diversity and inclusion.

This book calls for healing trauma through sharing stories because sharing stories allows us to relate to other life experiences. Sharing past traumatic experiences creates space for dialogue and maps new roads for moving from isolation to community engagement. Stories like this help us build new knowledge base that can be used in the healing process.

It is clear that at the initial stage, getting to know the stories of wounded women is key to any success in easing trauma. The power of social connections cannot be ignored in the process of healing. Unfortunately, for some reason immigrant and refugee service planning and delivery often makes it difficult for many immigrant and refugee women to access mainstream services. Therefore it is vital that professionals dedicate time to listen to immigrant and refugee women's stories so they are better able to construct paths to mainstream services using ethnic communities' organizations as cultural brokers.

I finish this book with the following quotes that guide me in my life. Mahatma Gandhi said "The best way to find yourself is to lose yourself in the service of others". Indeed, many people are continuing to lose themselves through helping others, a testimony to the progress of our humanity. In the same vein, Douglas Adam said that "To give real service you must add something which cannot be bought or measured with money, and that is sincerity and integrity". The women's stories shared and the tremendous work of unpaid caring for others by millions of women around the world is part of the strongest chain of human love that cannot be measured with money. I will continue to find ways to serve others, and I hope the stories in this book will help in that endeavor. My contribution as co-founder of Umoja Operation Compassion has been part of my loosing myself in the service of other immigrants and refugees.

References

Agnew, V. (Ed. 2007). *Interrogating Race and Racism.* Toronto: University of Toronto Press.

Ambrosini, V. & Bowman, C. (2001) Tacit knowledge: Some suggestions for operationalization. *Journal of Management Studies,* 38, 811-829.

Andersen, M. L. & Collins, P. H. (1995). Race, class, and gender. An anthology. Second edition. Belmont, CA: Wadsworth Publishing Company.

Basset, T., & Stickley, T. (2010). Voices of experience: narratives of mental health survivors. A John Wiley & Sons, Ltd., London.

Chow, W., Law, S., Andermann, L., Yang, J., Leszcz M, Wong, J. & Sadavoy, J. (2010). Multi-family psycho-education group for assertive community treatment clients and families of culturally diverse background: A pilot study. *Community Mental Health Journal* 46(4): 364-371.

Cortazzi, M. (2001) Narrative analysis in ethnography. In Atkinson, P., Coffey, A., Delamont, L. J.& Lofland, L. (Eds), *Handbook of Ethnography.* Thousand Oaks, CA., Sage.

Cox, T. J. (2001). *Creating the multicultural organization.* John Wiley & Sons Inc. New York, NY.

Creese, G. (2011). *The New African Diaspora in Vancouver: Migration, Exclusion and Belonging.* Toronto: University of Toronto Press.

Creese, G. (2010). Erasing English language competency: African immigrants in Vancouver, Canada. *Journal of International Migration and Integration,* 11(3): 295-313.

Creese, G. & Frisby, W. (Editors, 2011). *Feminist community research: Case studies and methodologies.* Vancouver: University of British Columbia Press.

Creese, G., & Kambere, E. N. (2003). What colour is your English? *The Canadian Review of Sociology and Anthropology.* 50(5), 565–573.

Creese, G., & Wiebe, B. (2009). Survival employment: Gender and deskilling among African immigrants in Canada. *International Migration.* 50: 56–76.

Diamond, A. (2010). The evidence base for improving school outcomes by addressing the whole child and by addressing skills and attitudes, not just content. *Early Education and Development*, 21, 780-793.

Donkor, M. (2000). *The education of immigrant women: prospects and challenges for Ghanaian immigrant women in Canada.* Unpublished Doctoral thesis. University of Toronto.

Dossa, P. (2004). *Politics and poetics of migration: Narratives of Iranian women from the Diaspora.* Toronto: Canadian Scholars Press Inc.

Dossa, P. (2002). Narrative mediation of conventional and new mental health paradigms: reading the stories of immigrant Iranian Women. *Medical Anthropology Quarterly*, 16(3): 341-359.

Edge, S., Newbold, K. B. & McKeary, M. (2014). Exploring socio-cultural factors that mediate, facilitate, & constrain the health and empowerment of refugee youth. *Social Science and Medicine*, 117: 34–41.

Este, D. & Bernard, W. T. (2006). Spirituality among African Nova Scotians: A key to survival in Canadian society. *Critical Social Work* 7(1): 1-22.

Fox, S. H. & Tang, S. S. (2000). The Sierra Leonean refugee experience: traumatic events and psychiatric sequelae. *Journal of Nervous Mental Diseases.* 188(8):490-5.

Herman, J. L. (1997). *Trauma and recovery: The aftermath of violence – from domestic abuse to political terror.* New York: Basic Books.

Hynes, M. & Lopes Cardozo, B. (2000). Observations from the CDC: Sexual Violence against Refugee Women, *Journal of Women's Health & Gender-Based Medicine*, 9(8): 819 -823.

James, M., Butcher, J. J., Halcon, L., Savik, K,. Spring, M. & Westermeyer, J. (2004). Somali and Oromo refugees: Correlates of torture and trauma history. *American Journal Public Health*. 94(4): 591–598

Favaro, A., Maiorami, M., Colombo, G. & Santonastaso, P. (1999). Traumatic experiences, post-traumatic stress disorder and dissociative symptoms in a group of refugees from former Yugoslavia (1999). *Journal of Nervous Mental Diseases*. 187(5): 306–308.

Keller, H., Voelker, S., & Yovsi, R. D. (2005). Conceptions of parenting in different cultural communities. The case of West African NGO and Northern German Women. *Social Development*, 14(1), 158-180.

Kitchen, P., Williams, A., & Chowhan, J. (2012). Sense of belonging and mental health in Hamilton, Ontario: an intra-urban analysis. *Social Indicators Research* 108, 277-297.

Linde, C. (2001). Narrative and social tacit knowledge. *Journal of Knowledge Management, Special Issue on Tacit Knowledge Exchange and Active Learning*, 5 (2), Retrieved on August 23, 2016 from:https://cseweb. ucsd.edu/~goguen/courses/papers/linde-narr-tacit.pdf

Masinda, M. T. & Ngene, E. K. 2008. Needs Assessment and Services Delivery Plan for African Immigrants and Refugees in Vancouver Metropolitan Area, British Columbia. Vancouver: United Way of the Lower Mainland and Umoja Operation Compassion Society.

Masinda, M.T. (2004). Impacts of colonial legacies and globalization processes on forced migration in modern Africa, *Research Review*, 20 (1), 18.

Mollica, R. (2006). *Healing invisible wounds: Paths to hope and recovery in a violent world*. Harcourt, New York.

Njenga, F. (2002). 'Focus on Psychiatry in East Africa'. *British Journal of Psychiatry* (181): 354-59.

Orphana, H. M., Lemyre, L. & Gravel, R. (2009). Income and psychological distress: The role of the social environment. *Health Reports* 20 (1). Ottawa: Statistics Canada.

Osteen, J. (2007). *Become a better you: 7 keys to improving your life everyday.* New York: Free.

Robert Schweitzer, Fritha Melville, Zachary Steel & Philippe Lacherez, Australian and New Zealand Journal of psychiatry 2006; 40: 179-187).

Piper, N. (2005). Gender and Migration: background paper for Global Commission on international migration (GCIM) and appendix to the GCIM Global Report on Migration, Recommendations to the Secretary General 14.

Pham, P.N., Weinstein, H. M. & Longman, T. (2004). Trauma and PTSD symptoms in Rwanda: implications for attitudes toward justice and reconciliation. *JAMA.* 292(5): 602-12.

Polanco-Roman, L. & Miranda, R. (2013). Culturally related stress, hopelessness, and vulnerability to depressive symptoms and suicidal ideation in emerging adulthood. *Behavior Therapy*, 44: 75-87.

Schweitzer, R., Melville, F., Steel, Z. & Lacherez, P. (2006). Trauma, post-migration living difficulties, and social support as predictors of psychological adjustment in resettled Sudanese refugees. *Australian and New Zealand Journal of Psychiatry*, 40: 179-187.

Silove, D. & Steel, Z. (2006). Understanding community psychosocial needs after disasters: implications for mental health services. *Journal of Postgraduate Medicine*, 52:121-125.

Trémolières, M. (ed. 2009). Regional challenges of West African Migration. African and European Perspectives. Paris. OECD.

Wasik, A. (2006). *Economic insecurity and isolation: Post-migration traumas among black African refugee women in the Greater Vancouver Area.* Working Paper Series No. 06-17. Vancouver, BC, Research on Immigration and Integration in the Metropolis.

www.ingramcontent.com/pod-product-compliance
Lightning Source LLC
Chambersburg PA
CBHW030432290526
45786CB00001B/255